Challenging Discriminatory Practices of Religious Socialization among Adolescents

"The world today is witnessing the emergence of religion as a disciplinary power regulating masses, democracies, and individuals. In this landmark work, Bhatia and Pathak-Shelat examine how adolescents are socialized as religious subjects in and through the major structures of governance. Based on their immersive work as media educators in villages of Gujarat, they have developed a counter-conduct framework to help young individuals challenge practices of religious discrimination in their communities. This counter-conduct framework uses media education as a site to design and practise forms of resistance. Something truly remarkable about this media education framework is its relevance at the global level. The framework is based on theoretical principles of learning and unlearning and can be applied to similar contexts wherein young individuals practice religious discrimination. The book combines theory with praxis to reveal ways in which adolescents can identify resources for resistance within themselves and their immediate media environments."
—Professor Sirkku Kotilainen, *Faculty of Information Technology and Communication, Tampere University, Finland*

"This book explores a research area largely untouched by media educators related to adolescents' engagement with their religious identities. The book provides an insightful understanding of how adolescents are socialized as religious subjects and are encouraged to enact their subjectivity by discriminating against the other. Based on this analysis, the book has made a pioneering contribution towards understanding how educators can design a Critical Media Education curriculum based on theoretical principles of dialogic engagement, applied theatre practices, inter-faith collaborations, spatial rearrangements, and content creation. It is going to be a valuable resource in several local and global societies where there is a need to challenge practices of religious discrimination and violence. The book could be a practical guide on how to use media education to enable the formation of inter-faith community living."
—Binod Agrawal, *Mentor, Media Research Center, MAHE, United Arab Emirates*

"In our troubled times, when religious identity has become less about developing a comfortable sense of the cultural self than a weapon to be used strategically against the Other, we need to understand how and why young people become socialized into difference. This book, drawing as it does on an intimate engagement with adolescents in villages in Gujarat, offers not only understanding but also a path to using these insights in fruitful ways. Given that media—along with a variety of other institutions—play a crucial role in building worlds and meanings, the critical media pedagogy outlined by the authors offers an opportunity and a means to break the cycle of misinformation and stereotyping that young people are often caught within. This book offers a lucid and compelling argument for engaging with adolescents from within their contexts and creating opportunities for critically questioning the dominant media discourse."

—Professor Usha Raman, *Department of Communication,*
University of Hyderabad, India

Kiran Vinod Bhatia · Manisha Pathak-Shelat

Challenging Discriminatory Practices of Religious Socialization among Adolescents

Critical Media Literacy and Pedagogies in Practice

Kiran Vinod Bhatia
School of Journalism and Mass
Communication
University of Wisconsin-Madison
Madison, United States

Manisha Pathak-Shelat
MICA
Ahmedabad, Gujarat, India

ISBN 978-3-030-29573-8   ISBN 978-3-030-29574-5   (eBook)
https://doi.org/10.1007/978-3-030-29574-5

Cover illustration: © Melisa Hasan

This Palgrave Pivot imprint is published by the registered company Springer Nature
Switzerland AG
The registered company address is: Gewerbestrasse 11, 6330 Cham, Switzerland

To our families, friends, and students...
We love you too!

FOREWORD

Any effort to trace the history of media literacy education is fraught, and yet some sense of this history is crucial to understand the innovative contribution to the field made by Bhatia and Pathak-Shelat's study, *Challenging Discriminatory Practices of Religious Socialization among Adolescents: Critical Media Literacy and Pedagogies in Practice.*

At a general level, media education has long been primarily concerned with the problem of meaning in media cultures: How meaning is constituted, by and for whom, and how mediated communication can be negotiated and contested, especially by those people and communities with the most at stake given the contingencies of power in media cultures. Williams' (1958) seminal analysis of the shifting meaning of five key words (industry, democracy, class, art, culture) in the history of modernity and everyday life in *Culture and Society* marked a decisive turning point for later work on media culture and media education. Williams' text [coupled with Hoggart's *Uses of Literacy* (1957)] influenced the development of British Cultural Studies and made clear how an understanding of the meaning and practices surrounding key terms can reveal the broader conditions and forces operating across socio-cultural life. These arguments influenced the writings of Paddy Whannel and Stuart Hall, and together with elements from McLuhan's medium theory and the influence of feminism and other social justice movements, the stage was set for the consolidation of media literacy key concept models in the 1980s and 1990s.

Masterman's *Teaching the Media* (1985) is undoubtedly the decisive text in defining and locating key concept models at the center of media education. While foregrounding representation as the central conceptual problematic for the field, Masterman drew on various core concepts from cultural studies to center media education around an investigation into (1) the sources and origins of media constructions, (2) the dominant codes used in media (3), the values embedded in media representations, and (4) the role of audiences in interpreting media. In each instance, questions of meaning were central to Masterman's framework. This work shaped the development of two influential versions of media literacy: the British Film Institute's list of concepts for primary and secondary education (Bazalgette 1989) and the Ministry of Ontario's list of eight key concepts (Jolls and Wilson 2014). These versions in turn became key resources for the development of media literacy education in a number of countries (i.e., Australia, the United States, South Africa, Finland, etc.) and within international organizations (i.e., UNESCO) in the 1990s and remain influential to this day.

In 2003, Buckingham's (2003) effort to define the focus and mark the accomplishments and challenges of media education situated key concepts in relation to the development of literacies. To do so, he narrowed the model down to four key concepts: production, language, representation, and audiences. Others, including Hoechsmann and Poyntz (2012), later articulated a project of digital media literacy that links together Richard Johnson's (1986–1987) key concepts in cultural studies with the 7-Cs (Consciousness, Communication, Consumption and Surveillance, Convergence, Creativity, Copy-Paste, and Community) of Media Literacy 2.0.

Over the past decade, the UNESCO Media and Information Literacy project has advanced an ambitious effort to develop policy and strategy guidelines and recommendations on media and information literacy for a remarkable range of national partners, government services, Internet and copyright regulators, educational jurisdictions and initiatives, industries, and local communities. The broad aim of the project is to develop a program to "enhance the creation of knowledge driven, inclusive, pluralistic, democratic and open societies (UNESCO *Media and Information Literacy Policy Strategy and Guidelines* 2013: 12). Toward these ends, media and information literacies are wed together to form a composite notion that recognizes and addresses the many ways information and media now shape people's lives. The project defines information literacy in relation to issues of information engagement "and the process of becoming informed. [Information literacy] is strongly associated with the concepts of learning to learn and making decisions [by] ... defining needs and problems" and the relevant information needed to act critically and responsibly (ibid., 47). Media literacy is about understanding "the nature ...[,] roles and functions of media and other information providers in society. Just as [with] information literacy, the [media literate] individual is able to critically analyze the content or information he or she encounters" (ibid., 47–48). These definitions are wed together to inform a composite concept that informs the knowledge, skills, and attitudes meant to enable citizens to learn, understand, act, access, and recognize information and media in a whole host of settings.

Debates about the meaning of media literacy education continue, but the larger point is that since at least the mid-1990s, the field of media literacy has evolved to become a global discourse made up of a complicated and sometimes contradictory array of practices, modalities, objectives, and traditions (McDougall 2014). These developments are no doubt a consequence of the globalization of communication systems and the intensification of consumerism among young people around the world. The result, however, has been an outpouring of policy discussions, policy papers, and pilot studies across Europe, North America, Asia, and other regions (Frau-Meigs and Torrent 2009). This has produced a complex field of media literacy practices and models, and it has led to a generalization and sometimes a de-politicization of the field in order that media education might be more seamlessly woven into disparate education systems (Poyntz 2015). As the proliferation of media literacies has been underway, a raft of new media forms and practices—including cross-media, transmedia, and spreadable media (Jenkins et al. 2013)—have encouraged the production of a myriad of discourses about "*digital* literacy, *new media* literacy [and] *transmedia* literacy" (McDougall 2014, 6). These and like developments have complicated and sometimes confused the meaning of media literacy education, thereby compounding the challenge of pinpointing alignments between youth media learning and mediated experience.

Into this context arrives Bhatia and Pathak-Shelat's exciting and provocative new study. Their work develops a unique and compelling approach to critical media literacy, largely inspired by the work of

Michel Foucault, in conjunction with a host of other media and literacy scholars. Their aim is ambitious: to address religious literacy, identity, community belonging, and social change. The context for this work is a group of young students in villages in Gujarat, most of whom it seems come into this study with entrenched and powerful forms of religious identity, built upon the exclusion and demonization of religious "others." The larger social context for this work is not only a long history of religious antagonism and bias, but a recent intensification in community divisions that has only deepened as a consequence of the larger political climate and recent history of community violence in India. This is an immensely challenging environment to pursue this project, and this along with quality of the media literacy intervention outlined in this work, only adds to the urgency of this book.

Challenging Discriminatory Practices of Religious Socialization among Adolescents offers a compelling introduction to the contemporary context driving religious antagonisms in Gujarat and the role of key media institutions in fostering antagonisms and antipathies toward religious "others." The ongoing tensions between Hindu and Muslim communities are obviously at the center of this divide, exemplified by the spatial organization and division within the communities and the modes of exclusion used by families, schools, the community at large, and local, regional, and political actors. This provides a deeply challenging and dangerous context in which to take up critical media literacy, and the authors are to be commended for their courage and willingness to engage some of the most deep-seated and violent forms of division within the community. The children, parents, and educators involved in this work are also to be commended for their willingness to explore connection and understanding, against a long history of division, ideology, and ignorance about the other.

The following text demonstrates a remarkable grasp of a range of critical influences in media education and the very helpful role Foucault's work on subjectification, technologies of the self and technologies of care, governmentality, and counter-practice can have in critical media education. There are few instances in our field where such a rich and complex array of sources have been brought together in a nuanced manner to inform the development of a media education project. Among other things, the use of Foucault enables the authors to address the spatial relationships that produce particular forms of religious identity and how to take on these conditions through reconstituted spatial relationships between students, their families, and their neighborhoods, rather than through a simple deconstruction of the meaning associated with specific bodies and places. I note this and suggest that the use of Foucault also helps the authors to address larger problematics linked to religious identity, including the fields of visibility that shape identities and specific regimes of knowledge, with the hope of initiating new forms of counter-conduct that open possibilities for novel subject identities among the young people in their study. This is an incredibly ambitious work, which is addressed through exciting, practitioner-ready activities and exciting learning scenarios that detail the experience and change in students' connections to each other.

The critical qualities of work are quite remarkable and hold the potential to make a significant contribution to the field of critical media education, not only in relation to theory, but more specifically, in relation to questions of religious identity and antagonism that are pronounced in many national contexts around the world. Bhatia and Pathak-Shelat's work does not ignore the problem of mediated meaning in children's lives, but their strategy is to explore the context and spatial conditions of students' experiences and relationships, in order to reroute these relationships toward experiences of connection, care, and consideration of the other. This is a remarkable and ambitious project, one that will shift the focus of media literacy education, particularly in those settings where the stakes for young people are highest and the difficulty of changing prospective futures is most acute.

Stuart R. Poyntz
Associate Professor
School of Communication
Simon Fraser University
Burnaby, Canada

REFERENCES

Bazalgette, C. (1989). *Primary media education: A curriculum statement.* London: British Film Institute.

Buckingham, D. (2003). *Media education: Literacy, learning and contemporary culture.* Cambridge: Polity Press.

Frau-Meigs, D., & Torrent, J. (2009). Media education policy: Toward a global rationale. In D. Frau-Meigs & J. Torrent (Eds.), *Mapping media education policies in the world* (pp. 15–21). New York: UN Alliance of Civilizations.

Hoechsmann, M., & Poyntz, S. (2012). *Media literacies: A critical introduction.* Chichester: Wiley-Blackwell.

Hoggart, R. (1957). *The uses of literacy.* Fairlawn: Essential Books.

Jenkins, H., Ford, S. & Green, J. (2013). *Spreadable media: Creating value and meaning in a network culture.* New York: New York UP.

Johnson, R. (1986–1987). What is cultural studies anyway? *Social Text, 16,* 38–80.

Jolls, T., & Wilson, C. (2014). The core concepts; Fundamental to media literacy yesterday, today and tomorrow. *Journal of Media Literacy Education, 6*(2), 68–78.

Masterman, L. (1985). *Teaching the Media.* London: Comedia Publishing Group.

McDougall, J. (2014). Media literacy: An incomplete project. In B. De Abreu & P. Mihailidis (Eds.), *Media literacy education in action: Theoretical and pedagogical perspectives* (pp. 3–10). New York: Routledge.

Poyntz, S. (2015). Conceptual futures: Thinking and the role of key concept models in media literacy education. *Media Education Research Journal, 6* (1), 63–79.

Williams, R. (1958). *Culture and society, 1780–1950.* New York: Columbia.

ACKNOWLEDGEMENTS

This book is an outcome of our commitment to the critical task of teaching and learning. Through our research, we strive to fulfill our obligation toward upholding moral principles of equality and peace; this book is a testimony of our efforts in this direction.

We wish to thank MICA, Ahmedabad—an institution of critical scholarship—for encouraging us to work with young individuals from rural communities in Gujarat. We are grateful to all our colleagues at MICA who helped us think through sensitive issues related to religious identities of our student participants. We would also like to thank Prof. Keval Kumar and Prof. Harmony Siganporia for reviewing the earliest drafts of this manuscript and providing crucial insights to substantiate our arguments.

Stuart R. Poyntz from the Simon Fraser University played a pivotal role in helping us create the theoretical backbone of this work by introducing us to critical theorists such as Foucault, Derrida, Bakhtin, and Lyotard. We will forever be grateful for his ingenious suggestions and feedback.

We would like to express our gratitude to the school authorities and village communities who supported our cause and work. Finally, our young research participants have nourished our minds with conversations and learning experiences which transcend the needs of this project. We will, forevermore, be indebted to them for enabling us with the critical competencies required to conceive and implement a project which intends to help others operate in the register of thought. Our students are our greatest teachers!

CONTENTS

LIST OF FIGURES

List of Tables

CHAPTER 1

Religion and Governmentality

Abstract In this chapter, we elaborate how religion operates as a social institution of governance and discipline in the society. We introduce our readers to the theory of governmentality by unpacking some key concepts such as the dominant rationality, macro- and micro-level of governance, regimes of knowledge and power, politics of truth, and others and elucidate these with empirical examples. The aim is to explain how the ideology of religious discrimination is circulated, reinforced, and reified by both the macro-systems of governance and everyday lived realities of individuals in societies.

Keywords Governmentality · Dominant rationality ·
Macro–micro-politics · Technologies of self · Regimes of
knowledge/power

INTRODUCTION

Today, religion is used to regulate physical spaces, communication networks, and content and national/local discourses in many parts of the world. Religion as a regulatory force is circulated through capillaries of everyday collective life, especially through education, media, and community living. Individuals make sense of and interact with the world from

© The Author(s) 2019   1
K. V. Bhatia and M. Pathak-Shelat, *Challenging Discriminatory*
Practices of Religious Socialization among Adolescents,
https://doi.org/10.1007/978-3-030-29574-5_1

within the interpretive boundaries established in and through the use of these capillaries of collective life. As the ideology of religious politics is circulated through and populates the central meaning-making systems of the society, an individual is socialized as a religious subject—he/she is disciplined to further the dominance of a particular ideology of governance and conduct in a society.

The raison d'etre of the ideology of religious politics is to produce power relations that enable a particular religious community to establish its cultural, political, and economic dominance in the state. This phenomenon results in the marginalization of the minority communities and causes a rift in the everyday interactions and affective associations of individuals from different religious groups. It is, therefore, crucial to define religion as a dominant regulatory force and examine how, instead of remaining a matter of private faith, it is circulated, reinforced, and reified through both social structures of governance and individual practices.

To develop a set of analytical practices useful for understanding how religion is imbricated with the structures of governance and acts as a regulatory system for disciplining individual bodies, we have deployed Foucault's theory of governmentality.

FORMATION OF A RELIGIOUS SUBJECT: GOVERNANCE AND CONDUCT

In this section, drawing from Foucault's work on governmentality, we identify the whole range of available techniques, practices, and discourses used to regulate the conduct of religious subjects. Analyzing this broad complex of thought, practice, and experience helps us examine governmentality as a theoretical force influencing the formation of a religious subject. Governmentality is defined as the theoretical force for examining how power (religion as a regulatory force in this work but other powers behave similarly) is diffused through everyday experiences; it is enacted through our participation, granted to, and exercised by individuals and institutions and not only the state. This is to say that for Foucault, power is embodied and enacted by a set of diverse forces, operating from a range of sites, rather than through state structures alone. Power is, thus, understood to be constitutive rather than simply coercive. Instead of simply limiting individual's ability to act (coercive), religion as a form of power and regulatory force enables subjects to act in particular ways and conduct themselves according to the prescribed religious guidelines (constitutive).

According to the theory of governmentality, there exists a semantic link between the governing, or what Foucault calls the "gouverner" (macroforces of power), and the modes of thinking and action adopted by individuals (micro-forces of power). Before we plunge into unpacking this argument, let us first understand the difference between the macro- and micro-forces of power.

1. Macro-forces of power: At the macro-level, we examine the larger structures of governance[1] such as the law making/implementing systems, media and communication technologies, government policies and plans, public infrastructure, national and local discourses influencing public sentiments, international policies/relations, and other systems established to regulate the conduct of the entire population. These systems of governance create guidelines and disciplinary mechanisms for the masses.
2. Micro-forces of power—At the micro-level, we examine the ways in which these meta-narratives and macro-systems of governance influence the everyday, associational experiences of individuals—how individuals interpret the guidelines of conduct coded by the larger regulatory forces for the entire population and shape their everyday practices accordingly.

According to this theory, when individuals work in conjunction with the governing structures—media, politics, education, and religion—and devise guidelines regulating their everyday interactions and practices such that the ideologies operating at the macro-level get reinforced, a dominant rationality emerges. Dominant rationality is the meaning-making system extensively used in a society. It is constituted of techniques of discipline created to enable individuals to regulate how they conduct themselves and others every day defined as technologies of the self. According to Foucault, technologies of the self are a group of techniques that "… permit individuals to affect by their own means or with the help of others a certain number of operations on their own bodies and souls so as to transform themselves in ways that allow them to attain a certain state of happiness, purity, wisdom,

---

[1] It is important to note here that governance doesn't imply the state and its administrative practices and policies. Governance, in this context, includes a wide range of social institutions, individuals, and forces which limit and inform the conduct of individuals in relation to others and the society.

perfection or immortality" (1997). Individuals use self-regulation strategies designed by individuals to govern their conduct in accordance with religious guidelines. These self-regulation strategies are called technologies of self.

Let us use an example to explain how the regulatory forces at the macrolevel shape the technologies of self used by individuals to regulate their conduct (Table 1.1).

As is illustrated in the example here, regulatory power and the dominant ideology infiltrate and constitute the self through various disciplinary techniques that shape and influence the everyday experiences of individuals (Foucault 2003). This is possible because the technologies of the self

Table 1.1   Macro–micro-analysis

Issue: Travel ban on Muslim immigrants from specific countries issued by the United States of America

Analysis

1. Macro-level: The executive order 13769 was in effect from January 27, 2017 to March 16, 2017 when it was superseded by the Executive Order 13780. Under this order, the U.S. Refugee Admissions Program was suspended for 120 days and included denying entry to Syrian refuges indefinitely. Under this order, the state was also instructed to suspend admission to citizens of countries (Iraq, Iran, Libya, Somalia, Sudan, Syria, and Yemen) which failed to meet the adjudication standards under U.S. immigration law for 90 days. Promoting the ideology of religious discrimination in public–political spaces as the dominant narrative (national and local discourse), deploying communication technologies and educational institutions to promote, validate, and reinforce this ideology, and creating laws to regulate the conduct of the masses in accordance with the politico-religious guidelines help in disciplining the population as a whole

2. Micro-Level: Individuals are socialized in and through these social institutions that promote the ideology of religious discrimination. As a result, individuals enact their religious identities by practicing forms of conduct that reinforce the dominant ideology. For instance, this executive order and the dominant ideology of discriminating against the Muslims in America emboldened violent practices due to the perceived political and legislative empowerment of the extremist elements in the state. In its most extreme form, this ideology manifests in the individual acts of bullying, racist attacks on Muslims, and the general all-encompassing Islamophobia in the world

It is important to note that bullying, racist attack, systemic exclusion, and other forms of extreme and violent acts are only one of the many techniques of disciplining the conduct of the "religious subject". Individuals devise several guidelines to conduct themselves, especially in relation to the religious other, and participate in reifying the dominant ideology of religious discrimination. These self-regulation techniques are defined as the technologies of self are developed under the dominant order and are standardized rules that include power differentials (Lemke 2001).

This gives rise to an interpretive realm or a meaning-making system with fixed horizon of possibilities. Within this realm, minor variations in interpretation and conduct are accommodated to the extent that these interpretive and/or experiential elements don't challenge the authority of the dominant ideology. The limits of this horizon of possibilities are fixed through the process of normalization wherein the state provides a predetermined guideline on what can be considered as normal conduct. Through the process of normalization, differences or deviance are identified and mitigated as threats for the healthy function of the society (Lallement 2014). The deviant individual is disciplined and/or punished and compelled to enact in accordance with the dominant rationality. In this case, the deviant body may either be the religious other or someone from within one's religious community who challenges and/or refuses to comply with the religious guidelines. Once the deviants are identified, violence—discursive and/or physical—is deployed to punish them and the act of disciplining the deviants is normalized.

This process of normalization operates at three levels:

a. Circulation—Religious guidelines detailing the premise for "normal conduct" are circulated in and through various channels of communication such as media, community interactions, educational institutions, legal and social regulations, and others.
b. Reification—Individuals are socialized to enact these guidelines and conduct themselves and others in accordance with the dominant rationality. The ideology of religious discrimination manifests in the form of prejudice and biases which translate into violence and aggression committed against the religious other.
c. Repetition—Once the premise of "normal conduct" is codified, disciplinary systems are created to compel individuals to enact it repetitively; any deviance from the normal conduct is punished and regulated.

Through these processes of circulation, reification, and repetition, a set of practices and forms of conduct are normalized. These normalized forms of conduct define the "politics of truth" in any given society.

According to Foucault, politics of truth constitute the types of discourses and forms of conduct accepted as truths in a society and the mechanism, techniques, and procedures deployed to enable these truths (discourses and conduct). For example, educational institutions are one of the many systems of governance which are used to socialize adolescents according to the dominant ideology. According to Banaji (2018), school curricula in some states of India are being rewritten to insert Hindutva ideology into the textbooks, reference material, and young adolescents' learning environments. Similarly, students in some madrasas are trained to enact their religious identities in radical and discriminatory ways—sometimes resulting in radicalized adolescents and/or individuals committing violence.

Many adolescents from both the communities are socialized, in one way or the other, to enact their religious identities by delineating how they are different from the religious other. Also, as these everyday practices, forms of conduct and thinking, are disseminated by legitimate social institutions and systems of governance, they are accepted by the local population, internalized, and become their truths.

The "politics of truth" in any given society can be examined at two levels:

1. Regimes of knowledge: At this level of analysis, the focus is on understanding how a space, phenomenon, or individual is perceived in a society. We identify the techniques and procedures used to make sense of the object of inquiry. The key question we ask at this level is What and how do we know about the object of inquiry? What and how (in what context) we know about an object of inquiry inform how we engage with it.
2. Regimes of practice: At this level of analysis, we unpack how individuals enact their engagement with objects of inquiry based on the regimes of knowledge they inhabit. The key question we ask while examining the regimes of practice is How do individuals participate in and enact the beliefs?

In order to understand how regimes of knowledge and practice emerge from and reinforce the "politics of truth," let us look at the following example (Table 1.2).

Within the dominant rationality of religious politics, power [appropriated by religious communities] circulates through and is reinforced and

Table 1.2 Regimes of knowledge and practice

Object of Inquiry: Ban on beef consumption
Regimes of knowledge: What and how do we know about the object of inquiry?

1. Hindu traditions: Cow is a revered animal and is considered to be a provider of food (milk) and sustenance
2. Politics (meat politics): Many political groups have used the issue of beef consumption and export as a political site to mobilize the Hindu votes. Under the pretext of protecting cows, and by implication the Hindu beliefs, these political groups have designed political campaigns to popularize the rhetoric of meat politics and gather support
3. Family/community tradition: If beef is a staple diet in the family and/or community then beef consumption is an everyday ritual and daily dietary need for some communities

Regimes of practice: How do people practice and enact their beliefs?

1. People may express solidarity and support the ban on beef consumption or may express discomfort on the basis of argument that consumption of beef is a dietary requirement/personal lifestyle choice
2. In some extreme cases, radicalized, far right, Hindu groups assume the role of "cow vigilantes" and lynch others, especially members of the religious and caste minorities, on the suspicion that the victims were either consuming or ferrying beef
3. Political parties may either propose new laws or amend the existing ones, making them more rigorous, to deter people from committing cow slaughter. In some cases where systems of governance legitimated by the state refuse to condemn brutal cases of lynching, it normalizes and validates actions inflicting violence on members of minority communities

---

reified through heterogeneous sites of socializations such as educational institutions, community interactions, media, family, and peer groups. In the following section, we identify the main sites of socialization and explain how these reinforce and reify the ideology of religious politics and the concomitant politics of truth and power relations.

SITES OF SOCIALIZATION

The central tenets of this study emerge from our immersive work as media educators in the state of Gujarat, India. In Gujarat, the ideology of religious politics and the emergent power relations between communities is circulated in and through heterogeneous locales of power. Here, locales of power are defined as sites and/or institutions of governance in and through which individuals are initiated into the dominant rationality, i.e., discriminating against the religious other. According to scholars such as Antal

(2008), Sud (2012), and Nussbaum (2007), media, educational institutions, and [religious] community life/interactions (everyday experiences), and local politics act as sites through which the power flows in the society (Fig. 1.1).

In Discipline and Punish (1997), Foucault emphasizes that these locales of power give rise to regulatory and disciplinary practices which are deployed to regulate the conduct of individuals and reinforce both the existing power relations and the dominant ideology. Regional media play a crucial role in informing the "worldview" of the people in Gujarat. The regional media—both mainstream and micro-level community media—defines ways in which the religious other is perceived, providing interpretive frameworks that resonate across social space. In an ethnographic study conducted by Bhatia (2016) in rural villages of Gujarat, many research participants [rural residents] claim that regional media reports news objectively. This claim, however, contrasts with this and several other studies conducted by Bhatia (2016, 2018), Jain (2010), and Ahmed (2010), which

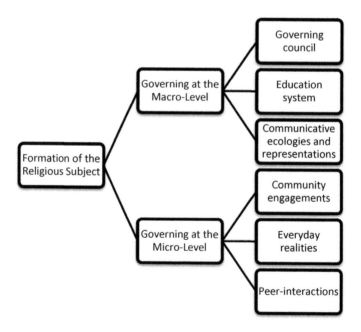

Fig. 1.1 Sites of socialization

suggest that the local Gujarati language-based mainstream media and some Urdu language periodicals are biased. Gujarati language-based periodicals often publish articles with an anti-Muslim and anti-Dalit (caste minority) narrative and reinforce the dominant ideology of discriminating against the minorities. For example, there are many instances wherein newspapers label a relationship between a Muslim man and a Hindu girl as an act of "love-jihad." This creates a deeper rift between different religious [also caste] communities and lessens the possibility of initiating inter-faith dialogues, understanding, and collaborations.

Beyond media representation, the regulatory power of religion also operates through educational institutions that work as material sites for constituting the collective psyche and generating a dominant frame for interpreting social realities in Gujarat. Besides the media/communication channels and educational institutions, community engagements and adolescents' lived realities of discrimination, injustice, depravation, and/or dominance play a key role in socializing them as religious subjects. In and through these lived realities and community experiences, adolescents learn to express their allegiance to their religious communities by performing specific tasks that are naturalized by the community—participation in religious activities, performance of rituals, prescribed use of language while referring to the religious other, and in some case engaging in acts of micro-aggression to hurt, dehumanize, disrespect, ostracize, and challenge the identity of the religious other. These activities open up religion to the performative realm and the political milieu.

The everyday lived realities are micro-practices of childhood and growing up; they are "tactics of everyday life" (de certeau 1984) and influence ways in which people engage with the religious other. These lived realities and community experiences are constituted of local systems of governance, families and peer groups, regional cultural practices, and everyday interactions. Through everyday experiences in their communities, adolescents address questions such as Who is the religious other? How am I different from the religious other? How should I behave while engaging with the religious other? As they are socialized in their communities, they learn to adopt forms of conduct in relation to their interactions and engagements with the religious other that are approved by and normalized in their communities which in most cases reinforce the differences between Hindus and Muslims and encourage adolescents to limit their interactions with each other. It is, however, also crucial to acknowledge there are several cases of children being socialized in learning environments wherein they are encouraged to develop and participate in inter-faith sites for strengthening communal ties in their communities. For instance, there are still many institutions, individuals, and ashrams such as *Madhi*, *Vedchhi* in *Bardoli*, *Babapur* near *Amereli*, *Anera*, and many others in Gujarat, probably more than any other state that is working relentlessly to preserve the secular ethos in the state.

It is clear by now that media, educational institutions, and community experiences (peer groups, family dynamics, local systems of governance, and cultural practices) act as sites through which the dominant rationality (religious politics) at the macro-level permeates the micro-realities of individuals, i.e., their everyday experiences, and ensures that they adopt technologies of self to conduct themselves in accordance with the existing politics of truth. The interface between macro-politics of regulatory power and the micro-politics of disciplinary power in communities takes place through these material sites and results in the formation of particular religious bodies.

In the absence of critical thinking skills and alternative forms of conduct, adolescents who are socialized as religious subjects practice discrimination and in some extreme cases use violence while engaging with the religious other. It is crucial that individuals are equipped with skills and experiences necessary to take an "interpretive detour" (Ricœur 1981) and analyze the "religious other" from beyond the limitations imposed by the predetermined religious identities and normalized forms of conduct.

Scholars such as Poyntz (2015), Bhatia and Pathak-Shelat (2017), and others suggest that media is an extremely crucial site within the broader framework of governmentality that serves as a regulatory force for managing both population and individual conduct. This is because media has the potential of leveraging a connection between what is happening at the macro-level (national discourse, public policies, political agendas, and others) and micro-realities of individuals such that people conduct themselves and others in accordance with the dominant rationality. The use of media, therefore, is both personal and public in nature. Though individuals use media in their personal lives and routines, through the consumption of narratives they connect with the larger political, socio-economic, and cultural issues. Also, when they insert media into their routines, they freely borrow interpretations and meanings circulated and disseminated through these organizations. Their engagements with media and the narratives, however, constitute the "freedom to choose" to either be influenced by the dominant rationality or to challenge/resist it. This brings us back to Foucault's conceptualization of power as a constitutive force which enables rather than enslaves people. In other words, the act of borrowing/accepting an interpretation/perspective submitted by the media (or any other social institution) is based on the premise that individuals have the right to choose or deny—to be conducted or not be conducted or be conducted in a different way. As a result, power is considered to be an enabling force that is situated in and with individual agency.

If we follow this theoretical delineation of power as a constitutive force, we can argue that individuals who choose to conduct themselves in accordance with the ideology of religious politics also have the agency to de-select it and develop alternative forms of conduct. In order to encourage individuals to practice resistance and challenge harmful forms of thinking and practice which are normalized through socialization processes, it is crucial to equip them with critical competencies. They must be enabled to examine and investigate discourses and practices of religious politics and if need be empowered to disrupt the normalized codes of conduct in relation to the religious other. There is a need to invigorate in individuals a will to re-examine their own interpretive frames and actions and invest these with new meanings based on ideas of inclusivity and cooperation.

According to Foucault (2007), this will of the individuals to decide "how to be conducted and how not to be conducted" such that resistance is contemporaneous with systems of power and dominance is defined as practices of counter-conduct. In other words, Foucault talks about a form of resistance that evaluates the system as a whole and looks for ways in which the existing "conditions of possibility" can be challenged to create alternate realities. In order to resist forces of governmentality, individuals must operate from within the system as religious subjects and citizens of India, using technologies of the self through which power is dispersed along the social field. It is here where resistance is possible using the same forces (media and education) through which regulation is imposed on religious bodies.

Individuals must be encouraged to question the authenticity of discriminatory practices normalized in their societies through the media discourses, community engagements (peer groups and family interactions), educational texts and teachings, and legitimate systems of governance. To equip adolescents with critical competencies required to question practices of religious socialization in their communities, we identify media education as a site of resistance wherein practices of counter-conduct can be developed.

CRITICAL MEDIA EDUCATION: A SITE FOR COUNTER-CONDUCT

Critical media education is conceptualized as a form of resistance to the constitutive work of systems of religious governmentality. According to Foucault's politics of resistance, processes of [religious] subject formation operate from multiple and heterogeneous locales, such as popular culture, including media representations and practices, traditional relations of authority and communal solidarities, including schools and educational institutions, individual experiences, societal expectations, and so on. According to many scholars, media play a central role in the socialization, acculturation, and the intellectual formation of young people (Bennett 2008; Buckingham 2003; Willet 2008; Hoechsmann and Poyntz 2012). If young people are educated about how political and cultural forces work through media to influence the exercise of power in the society, it can foster critical and equitable participation in public life. Critical media education can appropriate mediated spaces as sites of resistance that upend societal hierarchies. In this conceptualization of critical media education, we begin with the assumption that the religious subjects on whom the forces of disciplinary technologies are enacted are replete with capacities (Patton 1989) to understand and reinforce this political rationality. Here, critical media education is understood as a set of pedagogic strategies to encourage adolescents to challenge power relations by identifying resources for resistance within themselves and their immediate media environments by participating in the analytics of problematization. Critical media education is focused on the task of problematizing the historical conditions on which the identity of a religious subject is based by disturbing the narratives, practices, and spaces that reinforce the dominant rationality. It can be identified as a set of intervention strategies designed to produce a rapid mutation of events, to use taken-for-granted media spaces to enact different realities, and to question the common sense underlying historical narratives. Critical media education encourages a perpetual vigilance and skepticism regarding the reality-and-truth function of the self, the government, media, and society more generally.

CONCLUSION

The ontological force of the project of critical media education and the task of problematization rests in exploring the "present" and who "we" are in it. This process involves unpacking how the normalized conditions of possibility limit the ways in which we conduct ourselves and others as religious subjects. In identifying this constitutive power of religion, individuals can be encouraged to transcend the limits and conceive new modes of being and conduct.

In the words of Foucault (1988), "… such a project has to be conceived as an attitude, an ethos, a philosophical life in which the critique of what we are is at one and the same time the historical analysis of the limits that are imposed on us and an experiment with the possibility of going beyond them." The focus of our work was to help adolescents identify the limits of who they are, how they are socialized as religious subjects, and how the process of socialization influences their thoughts and actions. In the following chapters, we describe this approach at length and explain how we created the critical media education pedagogy to develop inter-faith sites for dialogue, participation, and collaboration among adolescents from the Hindu and Muslim communities in villages of Gujarat.

REFERENCES

Ahmed, S. (2010). The role of the media during communal riots in India: A study of the 1984 Sikh riots and the 2002 Gujarat riots. *Media Asia, 37*(2), 103–111.

Antal, C. (2008). Reflections on religious nationalism, conflict and schooling in developing democracies: India and Israel in comparative perspective. *Compare: A Journal of Comparative and International Education, 38*(1), 87–102.

Banaji, S. (2018). Vigilante publics: Orientalism, modernity and Hindutva fascism in India. *Javnost, 25*, 33–350.

Bennett, W. L. (2008). Changing citizenship in the digital age. In W. L. Bennett (Ed.), *Civic life online: Learning how digital media can engage youth* (pp. 1–24). Cambridge: MIT Press.

Bhatia, K. (2016). Understanding the role of media education in promoting religious literacy: A critical pedagogy for primary school students in rural India. *Media Education Research Journal, 7*(2), 11–28.

Bhatia, K. (2018). Mediating religious literacy among primary school children in Gujarat: Classrooms as a liminal space. *Journal of Media Literacy Education, 10*(3), 152–170.

Bhatia, K., & Pathak-Shelat, M. (2017). Media literacy as a pathway to religious literacy in pluralistic democracies: Designing a critical media education pedagogy for primary school children in India. *Interactions: Studies in Communication & Culture, 8*(2), 189–209.

Buckingham, D. (2003). *Media education: Literacy, learning and contemporary culture*. Cambridge: Polity Press.

de Certeau, M. (1984). *The practices of everyday life*. Los Angeles: University of California Press.

Foucault, M. (1988). Technologies of the self. In L. H. Martin, H. Gutman, & P. H. Hutton (Eds.), *Technologies of the self: A seminar with Michel Foucault* (pp. 16–49). London: Tavistock.

Foucault, M. (1997). *Discipline and punish: The birth of the prison* (A. Sheridan, Trans.). New York: Random House.

Foucault, M. (2003). *'Society must be defended': Lectures at the Collège de France 1975–1976*. New York: Picador.

Foucault, M. (2007). *Security, territory, population: Lectures at the Collège de France 1977–1978*. Basingstoke: Palgrave Macmillan.

Hoechsmann, M., & Poyntz, S. (2012). *Media literacies: A critical introduction*. Chichester: Wiley-Blackwell.

Jain, A. (2010). Beaming it live: 24-hour television news, the spectator and the spectacle of the 2002 Gujarat carnage. *South Asian Popular Culture, 8*(2), 163–179.

Lallement, M. (2014). Foucault's biopolitics: A critique of ontology. *Journal of the British Society for Phenomenology, 43*(1), 76–91.

Lemke, T. (2001). The birth of biopolitics: Michel Foucault's lecture at the Collège de France on neo-liberal government. *Economy and Society, 30*, 190–207.

Nussbaum, M. (2007). *The clash within: Democracy, religious violence, and India's future*. Cambridge: Harvard University Press.

Patton, P. (1989). Taylor and Foucault on power and freedom. *Political Studies, 37*(2), 260–276.

Poyntz, S. (2015). Conceptual futures: Thinking and the role of key concept models in media literacy education. *Media Education Research Journal, 6*(1), 63–79.

Ricœur, P. (1981). *Hermeneutics and the human sciences*. Cambridge: Cambridge University Press.

Sud, N. (2012). *Liberalization, Hindu nationalism and the state: A biography of Gujarat*. New Delhi: Oxford University Press.

Willet, R. (2008). Consumer citizens online: Structure, agency, and gender in online participation. In D. Buckingham (Ed.), *Youth, identity and digital media* (pp. 49–69). Cambridge: MIT Press.

CHAPTER 2

Methods and Analysis

Abstract In this chapter, we provide a rich description of the research site and the methodology which guided this research. We have developed an ethnographic approach to participatory action research in this project, and this framework draws its theoretical force from the concept of communicative ecology. We argue that in examining children's media engagements and how these influence them, it is important to develop culturally sensitive methodologies of data collection and intervention. We also reflect on the challenges of developing an ethnographic and participatory approach to conducting action research with children from vulnerable background. This chapter offers a methodological framework which can be deployed by other researchers and educators with minor modifications for conducting similar studies.

Keywords Ethnography · Participatory practices · Action research · Communicative ecology · Community immersion · Media educators

INTRODUCTION

According to the World Development Report (2019), despite a steady rise in the number of users, Internet is inaccessible to a majority of the world's population. Out of the 7.7 billion global populations, only 4.39 billion

© The Author(s) 2019   15
K. V. Bhatia and M. Pathak-Shelat, *Challenging Discriminatory
Practices of Religious Socialization among Adolescents*,
https://doi.org/10.1007/978-3-030-29574-5_2

have access to the Internet. In countries of global south, many people have no access to Internet and lie outside the range of mobile network coverage.

Most of the current Western studies and several from the global south in the area of media education, however, focus on the potential of digital technologies and develop concepts and theories to explore digital cultures (Bakardjieva 2010; Jenkins et al. 2016; Lemish 2015).

We acknowledge that these studies help researchers and academicians raise important questions related to the highly digital and mediatized learning environments of adolescents and also provide important insights into designing digital literacy programs. The emphasis to explore the dynamics of the digital media–adolescents collocation, however, draws attention away from the diminishing scholarly interest in the lived realities of young adolescents in non-digital cultural contexts and an under-representation of their concerns. Very few studies (Banaji 2015; Pathak-Shelat and Deshano 2013; Rangaswamy et al. 2008) explore and analyze how adolescents' compliance with social structures and norms influences their engagement with media.

In this book, we focus on how religion as a social institution plays a role in this process, especially in relation to adolescents for whom digital media are not the dominant channels of communication in their media ecologies. We propose that media cultures of adolescents who have limited access to media technologies and rely on community networks to forge relations are highly situated in a set of social, political, and cultural dynamics characteristic of their local everyday experiences, and it is important to examine these everyday experiences for designing meaningful media education programs for these adolescents. In India, for instance, a large number of young adolescents still rely more on traditional physical spaces to forge social ties and develop communication networks. In order to explore their media cultures, it is important to decenter technology and pay attention to various elements such as community relations, family dynamics, school interactions, and social structures (*sites of socialization*) which play an important role in the social construction of childhood experiences.

The purpose of this book is twofold. First, we examine how adolescents are raised as religious subjects in and through the several sites of socialization. This theoretical collocation of the sites of socialization and the process of [religious] subject formation are explored within the framework of communicative ecologies. Second, based on our analysis of adolescents' communicative ecologies, we develop the critical media education pedagogy that will help students question, challenge, and upend power hierarchies and inter-religious relations in their communities. In doing this, we utilize media cultures as "a site of pedagogy" (Hoechsmann and Poyntz 2012) and develop appropriate strategies to explore how media acts as a cultural text and operates through a complex network of formative technologies, institutions, practices, conduct, and ideas. This can shape and open up possibilities enabling media educators to repurpose mediascapes as resources for learning and civic engagement.

RESEARCH SITES

The data informing the arguments in this book were collected from three villages[1] located in the westernmost *tehsil* of the Ahmedabad district in the state of Gujarat. These villages have a total population of 4800 registered voters as per the 2016 voting list submitted by the *Gram Panchayat*.[2] Residents in these villages follow either the Hindu or the Muslim religion. They also follow a caste system according to which residents are segregated as members of the upper caste and the lower caste; the caste system is considered to be extremely important within the Hindu community of these villages.

According to the 2016 voting list, there are 1900 upper-caste Hindu households, 500 lower-caste Hindu households, and 1200 Muslim households in these villages. Religion and caste identities play a key role in influencing the associational life and everyday interactions among the village residents. An interesting example reflecting how religious and caste identities influence inter-faith/caste interactions among residents is the segregation of residential areas on religious and caste lines. In these villages, Muslim residential areas are constructed on the margins and around the main mosque, while the Hindu households are built closer to the village center, near the temple grounds. As is evident, religious identities have shaped the material, spatial, and communication environments in these villages, typical of Indian rural areas.

---

[1]We have used pseudonyms for all the villages included as research sites in our work. As the study deals with the topic of religious politics and discriminatory practices, it is crucial to protect the study participants from any untoward harm and/or threats.

[2]A *Gram Panchayat* (village council) is a formalized system of local self-governance in the villages and smaller towns of India. It is headed by a *sarpanch* who is the elected representative from the village/town.

Young individuals in these villages are socialized according to the dominant politico-religious guidelines which operate at two levels:

a. At the macro-level, adolescents engage with meta-narratives detailing guidelines on how to conduct oneself and/or be conducted as a religious subject. At this level, individuals are governed by laws, national and local discourses, and social institutions, all delineating answers to the question What does it mean to be a Hindu/Muslim in a particular context, here Gujarat? Analysis at this level requires examining how religious guidelines are subsumed in the structures of governance (laws, education, political rights) in order to regulate the conduct of individuals.

b. At the micro-level, we unpack ways in which these meta-narratives influence the everyday, associational experiences of individuals from different religious communities who work, live, and study together. At this level of analysis, we make efforts to address questions such as How do individuals engage with the religious other? How do individuals enact their religious identities in and through their everyday interactions? How can scholars, researchers, and policy makers create inter-faith sites and encourage people to negotiate with their biases toward the religious other?

Based on this two-step analysis, we argue that socializing individuals as religious subjects who are trained to perpetuate violence and/or discriminate against the religious other is a complex process. Examining this process requires that we pay attention to the ways and channels through which the ideology of religious politics is circulated at the macro-level and permeates the lived realities of individuals at the micro-level.

For this, we had to first explore communicative ecologies of adolescents in these villages to examine the potential of the social networks they inhabit in governing them as religious subjects, and help them identify the limits imposed by this process of subjectification on the emergence of other possible forms of knowledge, action, and "being." Later, in order to make intelligible the limits of who they are, how they are socialized as religious subjects, and how it influences their thoughts and actions, adolescents were introduced to critical practices of engagement through media education exercises designed for them. We combined two research approaches, i.e., ethnography and participatory action research, to develop a methodology that allowed us to answer the following research questions:

1. What is the role of religion in the formation of the religiously governable subjects?
2. How do media and education contribute as sites that enforce regulatory practices of governance on religious bodies?
3. How can critical media education encourage practices of counter-conduct to provoke forms of resistance among religious subjects?

We used ethnographic immersion and participation to study the process of "subjectification" of adolescents and identify channels used to govern them as religious subjects. We used principles of action research to develop critical media education exercises which would enable adolescents to investigate their subjectivities and challenge unassumed religious identities. Also, we relied on participatory methods to ensure that adolescents co-created media education exercises and owned this process of resistance.

Developing an Ethnographic Approach to Study the Communicative Ecologies of Adolescents

Debates over adolescents' interactions with media and socialization have repeatedly surfaced since the advent of technologies of mass communication in the nineteenth century. Many studies argue that the presence of media technologies in the lives of adolescents has transformed their childhood experiences. For instance, studies indicate that adolescents are negotiating their identities in interaction with their media experiences (Avila-Saavedra 2013), they are getting older faster (Hoechsmann and Poyntz 2012; Livingstone 2009) as they are exposed to mature content, they are revitalizing the markets by articulating their role as consumers of products (Hill 2011), and they are using media technologies for various entertainment and education purposes (Livingstone and Haddon 2009). Any work concerning adolescents' mediated life, however, cannot be wholly ensnared in debates about media's effects on adolescents and must take into account factors and circumstances which combine to explain adolescents' media experiences.

Adolescents use different socio-cultural resources, draw from their lived experiences and engage with media texts from within the interpretive boundaries of meaning-making practices abstracted from their communities, families, and friends. It is, thus, crucial that studies exploring adolescents' media cultures unveil the productive associations between the structural elements and personal experiences by effectuating conversations about their lived realities. Analyzing adolescents' media culture begins by positioning it in relation to other cultural dimensions and social relations (Meyrowitz 1984).

In this research, we identify theoretical concepts and develop a methodological approach which will help researchers examine adolescents' media cultures in similar contexts. In this analysis, we have used the concept of "communicative ecology" to uncover the links between the social structures and media practices of adolescents.

Communicative Ecology

Communicative ecology is an analytical framework deployed in the area of media studies and research in order to examine the linkages between material channels of communication, social structures, and cultural realities in a society. This concept was introduced by Altheide (1994) who argued that communication is a reflexive activity and media experiences are instituted by a range of techniques, tools, technologies, social structures, relations, and realities which contribute to specific interpretive and constructive frames. In other words, he proposes a sensitizing concept, ecology of communication, for combining everyday realities with a host of communication channels to develop a perspective on how social life is a communicated experience where media act as one of the many factors contributing to reinforce the rules and logic of any sphere of experience. The ecology of communication, therefore, comprises mutually influential relationships between information technologies, communication formats, social realities, cultural practices, and individual experiences.

According to several other scholars (Davison et al. 2014; Foth and Hearn 2007), studies exploring communicative ecologies must propose to conduct an analysis at three levels, i.e., the technological level, the social level, and the discursive level (Fig. 2.1).

Examining the *technological layer* helps identify various channels of communication, media technologies, techniques of interactions, and tools of information circulation and gathering that constitute media experiences of individuals in a given society. In the three villages we studied, for instance, the various media and communication technologies, tools and techniques

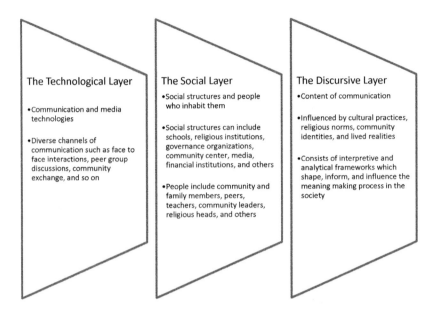

Fig. 2.1 Examining the communicative ecologies: three level analysis

which form this layer include newspapers, television, radio, mobile phones, community interactions, exchange of ideas in peer circles, guidelines issued by school authorities, instructions of conduct given by family members, and social expectations guiding adolescents' everyday conduct articulated through channels of governance such as the village *Panchayat*, community elders, and religious leaders. These channels of communication relay information about cultural norms, social codes of conduct, and societal expectations to individuals who occupy and make use of these communicative spaces.

People animate these channels of communication and give meaning to these systems of technologies. By adhering to and practicing the dominant rationality, media and communication technologies are appropriated by the residents of the village in order to shape and reify meaning-making processes which revitalize the village communities and social relations. Examining the *social layer* helps understand the interrelatedness of media spheres and the lived realities of people in these villages. For instance, adolescents in these villages often attend religious classes curated for them by religious leaders who use mosques and temples/community halls as communication platforms to socialize adolescents in accordance with their worldviews. These classes account for how adolescents practice childhood within specific temporally and spatially situated contexts. Religious leaders socialize adolescents into adopting particular frames for interpreting their interactions, experiences and socio-cultural realities, and the ways which reinforce the truth claims of their respective communities. These frames of interpretation define the content of communication which circulates through the society.

It is important to note that meaning is not contained within cultural works but is disseminated through audience as the discursive work of the interpretive community (Fish 1980). The *discursive layer*, therefore, is primarily "… our language and penchant for analysis that leads us to focus on certain moments in a process and split them off for investigation" (Altheide 1994). In other words, it examines how individuals use language to make sense of the social realities and their everyday experiences.

We used this triple-layered communicative ecology framework in our work to examine the flow of information in the lives of adolescents in these villages. We focused our analysis on unpacking how adolescents receive information (forms, channels, and formats), how they analyze and interpret their media engagements, and how they translate the meanings they derive from these media engagements into everyday practices.

Data Collection

In order to collect data for these dimensions, we started working as media educators at the only municipal Primary School in these three villages. For this, we procured permissions from the Primary School Board (*Prathmik Shala Kendra*) in Ahmedabad, took the school community into confidence, and started conducting 40 minutes of media education classes in the school for students from grades 6 to 8, three times every week. This helped us develop a rapport with the students and through them gain access to their village communities.

We used two ethnographic methods, i.e., participant observations and semi-structured in-depth interviews in various places such as households, community spaces, streets, temples, mosques, shops, and classrooms. For conducting interviews, we asked student participants if their families would be interested in participating in the study. Out of the 80 students we approached, families of 40 students agreed to meet us and receive more information about the interview process, i.e., the objectives, procedure, involvement requirements, and so on.

We conducted interviews with 37 families and 129 adolescents to understand their communicative ecologies. The interview schedule had questions related to the history of the village, interactions between different religious communities, political apparatus prevalent in the village, types of cultural spaces in the villages which the residents routinely use and occupy, educational infrastructure and opportunities, media habits, communication channels and spaces, and their political ideology.

The transcripts were analyzed using thematic analysis (Braun and Clarke 2006), and the second round of interviews was conducted to seek further clarifications on specific issues and ideas.

Along with adults, we also interviewed 129 adolescents during our two years of work as media educators in the primary school that caters to the educational needs of adolescents from three villages in the Ahmedabad district in Gujarat. We started working with 150 adolescents of grade six, seventh, and eighth in 2015 and have since been involved in their everyday experiences in the role of their teachers. Interviews with adolescents were mostly conducted in their classrooms during their free time and lasted for about 30 minutes. We interspersed our interview data with participant observations (Williamson and Brown 2014) to examine the processes and channels through which adolescents were socialized as religiously governable subjects. For this, we immersed in their village communities and explored the material, spatial, and ideological dimensions of their communicative ecologies.

Our analysis of the resulting ethnographic data revealed an urgent need for developing a media education initiative which would equip students with critical competencies necessary to challenge the dominant narratives, routinized social identities, and normalized life experiences of receiving and meting out discrimination. What young people need in such times of religious prejudices and social inequalities in these villages is a way to resist the dominant structures of power and transgress social norms.

With this in mind, we designed an action research project to develop critical media education program for and with the students as a form of resistance to the constitutive work of systems of religious governmentality. Critical media education program was designed to help adolescents appropriate mediated spaces as sites of resistance and challenge and/or ruffle the societal hierarchies and dominant rationality.

In this book, critical media education is understood as a set of pedagogic strategies to encourage adolescents to practice what Dean calls the analytics of problematization and in doing that challenge power relations by identifying resources for resistance within themselves and their immediate media environments. In order to design this intervention, we borrowed elements of ethnographic research methods including long-term engagement and immersion in village communities to understand the local contexts historically. We used participatory monitoring and evaluation methodology (Lennie and Tacchi 2013) to analyze the various media education exercises designed in terms of their local situatedness and relevance to the everyday experiences of adolescents in these villages.

We used this multiple-method approach to examine the everyday life of adolescents constituted of "… different communicative resources which messily combine or conflict with some entities but block others" (Slater 2013). There are five elements underpinning this methodology—participatory practices, contextual learning, prolonged immersion, critical competencies, and multiple iterations (Fig. 2.2). Each of these five elements has been defined as under:

1. Participatory practices: For a research design to be truly inclusive participants must be involved at all the stages of research—right from conceptualizing the research problem, collecting data, designing and implementing intervention, evaluating the project, revamping strategies, and monitoring progress. We encouraged students to identify issues that hindered their classroom interactions with other students, we helped them voice their concerns in the form of text-based, audio, or video narratives, and included them in ideating media education exercises.

2. Contextual Learning: We immersed in their community life, frequented their village spaces and houses, participated in their community functions and worked as media educators for two years in order to understand their socio-cultural, political, and religious realities. We relied on students, school teachers, and community members to introduce us to their cultural practices and everyday realities as we acknowledge their place of authority in this scheme of interactions and experiences.

3. Prolonged Immersion: From studying their media cultures, understanding the historical conditions sustaining their social structures, to exploring their cultural norms, we had to engage with the participants

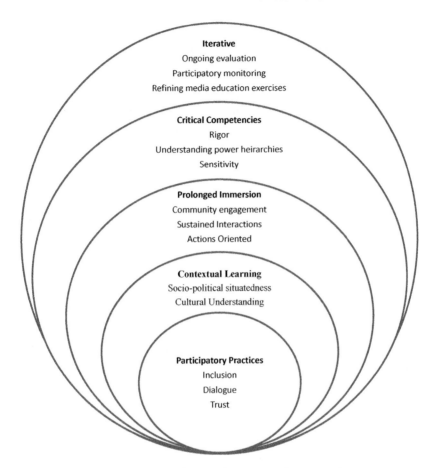

Iterative
Ongoing evaluation
Participatory monitoring
Refining media education exercises

Critical Competencies
Rigor
Understanding power heirarchies
Sensitivity

Prolonged Immersion
Community engagement
Sustained Interactions
Actions Oriented

Contextual Learning
Socio-political situatedness
Cultural Understanding

Participatory Practices
Inclusion
Dialogue
Trust

Fig. 2.2   Ethnographic approach to participatory action research

at length and become an outsider who had access to an insider role while visiting the community.

4. Critical Competencies: This element guides the role of both the researcher and the participants. As media educators-cum-researchers, we used theoretical tenets provided by scholars of critical education (Freire 1973; Giroux 1992; Lankshear 1997; McLaren 1995) in order

to create a learning environment which encourages students to question the taken-for-granted social structures without necessarily disrupting the authority (Velde 2012).

5. Iterative Process: All these elements evolve and play out in the research process simultaneously as they complement the development of research practices, methods, tools, and interventions all at once. For instance, while designing media education exercise based on ethnographic narratives of adolescents' media cultures, the researcher and participants have to constantly monitor the effectiveness of a media education program, build on and nourish students' capacities to engage with the processes, collect more data from the village communities to make the programs locally relevant, and involve community members in these processes to ensure that the program is owned by them.

These elements briefly capture the processes involved in examining adolescents' media cultures in villages of Gujarat with an intention of introducing changes that would enrich their media experiences and enable them to critically enact their social roles and religious identities in personal and public spaces.

In the next chapter, we investigate the analytics of governance in these villages and how it contributes to the formation of a religious subject.

References

Altheide, D. L. (1994). An ecology of communication: Toward a mapping of the effective environment. *The Sociological Quarterly, 35*(4), 665–683.

Avila-Saavedra, G. (2013). Neither here nor there: Consumption of US media among pre-adolescent girls in Ecuador. *Interactions: Studies in Communication & Culture, 4*(3), 136–152.

Bakardjieva, M. (2010). The internet and subactivism: Cultivating young citizenship in everyday life. In T. Olsson & P. Dahlgren (Eds.), *Young people, ICTs, and democracy: Theories, policies, identities and websites* (pp. 129–146). Goteborg, Sweden: Nordicom, University of Gothenburg.

Banaji, S. (2015). Behind the high-tech fetish: Children, work and media use across classes in India. *The International Communication Gazette, 77*(6), 577–599.

Braun, V., & Clarke, V. (2006). Using thematic analysis in psychology. *Qualitative Research in Psychology, 3*(2), 77–101.

Davison, R. M., Ou, C., Martinsons, M., Zhao, A., & Du, R. (2014). The communicative ecology of Web 2.0 at work: Social networking in the workspace. *Journal of the Association for Information Science and Technology, 65*(10), 2035–2047.

Fish, S. (1980). *Is there a text in this class.* Cambridge, UK: Harvard University Press.

Foth, M., & Hearn, G. (2007). Networked individualism of urban residents: Discovering the communicative ecology in inner-city apartment buildings. *Information, Communication & Society, 10*(5), 749–772.

Freire, P. (1973). *Education for critical consciousness.* New York, NY: Seabury Press.

Giroux, H. A. (1992). *Border crossings: Cultural workers and the politics of education.* New York: Routledge.

Hill, J. (2011). Endangered childhoods: How consumerism is impacting child and youth identity. *Media, Culture and Society, 33*(3), 347–362.

Hoechsmann, M., & Poyntz, S. (2012). *Media literacies: A critical introduction.* Chichester: Wiley-Blackwell.

Jenkins, H., Shresthova, S., Gamber-Thompson, L., Kligler-Vilenchik, N., & Zimmerman, A. (2016). *By any media necessary: The new youth activism.* New York; NY: New York University Press.

Lankshear, C. (1997). *Changing literacies, changing education.* New York: Open University Press.

Lemish, D. (2015). *Children and media: A global perspective.* Oxford: Wiley Blackwell.

Lennie, J., & Tacchi, J. (2013). *Evaluating communication for development: A framework for social change.* Abingdon: Routledge.

Livingstone, S. (2009). *Children and the internet: Great expectations, challenging realities.* Cambridge: Polity Press.

Livingstone, S., & Haddon, L. (2009). *Young people in the European digital media landscape: A statistical overview.* Goteborg, Sweden: International Clearinghouse on Children, Youth and Media.

McLaren, P. (1995). *Critical pedagogy and predatory culture: Oppositional politics in a postmodern era.* New York, NY: Routledge.

Meyrowitz, J. (1984). The adultlike child and the childlike adult: Socialization in an electronic world. *Daedalus, 113*(3), 19–48.

Pathak-Shelat, M., & DeShano, C. (2013). Digital youth cultures in small town and rural Gujarat, India. *New Media and Society, 16*(6), 983–1001.

Rangaswamy, N., Nair, S., & Toyama, K. (2008). "My TV is the family oven/toaster/grill": Personalizing TV for the Indian audience. In *Proceeding of the 1st International Conference on Designing Interactive User Experiences for TV and Video—uxtv '08.* Silicon Valley, CA, USA.

Slater, D. (2013). *New media, development and gobalization: Making connections in the global south.* Cambridge: Polity Press.

Velde, J. (2012). *From liminal to liminoid: Eminem's trickstering.* Bergen: University of Bergen.

Williamson, K. M., & Brown, K. (2014). Collective voices: Engagement of Hartford community residents through participatory action research. *The Qualitative Report, 19*(36), 1–14.

CHAPTER 3

Analytics of Governmentality and Formation of the Religious Subject

Abstract In this chapter, we present insightful conversations with and among school students and residents of the villages to explicate the ways in which macro-forces of power permeate and influence the everyday realities of adolescents in these villages. We argue that macro-politics percolate into the lived experiences of individuals through both discursive and non-discursive channels that are sustained by routinized practices of everyday rituals such as education, punishment, communication, participation, worship, and showing allegiance. We explain how the dominant rationality of religious politics shapes the political reality of the subjects with the help of regulatory techniques and moral arguments.

Keywords Macro-politics · Micro-politics · Technologies of self · Religious subject · Schools · Communities · Institutions of governance

March 17, 2016

We were waiting for eighth grade students to return to their brightly lit classroom after their lunch break. As we sat at the table, Seema and Priya[1]

---

[1] The real names of participants of my study have not been revealed in order to protect them from any possible threat.

© The Author(s) 2019   29
K. V. Bhatia and M. Pathak-Shelat, *Challenging Discriminatory Practices of Religious Socialization among Adolescents*,
https://doi.org/10.1007/978-3-030-29574-5_3

entered the classroom and started discussing the India versus Pakistan T20 match from the previous evening. They were excited that India had won the match and were giggling about "how cute Kohli[2] is" just when Razia, a Muslim student, joined the conversation and expressed how she was in love with Kohli. Let us look at the conversation:

> *Priya*: You can't like Kohli! Your team lost because of him! Hahah...
> *Razia (expressing disbelief)*: My team lost? Really? But India won the match, isn't it?
> *Priya (still giggling)*: Of course India won because it defeated your team, right?
> *Razia (turning red with embarrassment)*: What do you mean?
> *Seema (trying to provide an explanation)*: Aree, she is just kidding. You are a *Musalman* so we thought you support the Pakistani cricket team... that is why we...

(Seema and Priya started giggling as Razia walked toward her seat at the end of the classroom).

This example is illustrative of one of the many ways in which the ideology of religious politics seeps into the everyday experiences of students through community interactions, media consumption, and classroom education/experiences. As is evident, adolescents' experiences in these villages are influenced by a complex interaction between the dynamics of global, national, and state politics and their engagements in the immediate community. They are socialized by families who raise them within binaries such as self/other and Hindu/Muslims (Bhatia 2016; Bhatia and Pathak-Shelat 2017), are exposed to a an ideology of religious discrimination prevalent in regional media channels (Ahmed 2010; Jain 2010; Rajagopal 2001), are raised in a tradition of religious teachings which portray differences as abnormalities and promote ideas of "purity" (Sikand 2008; Sud 2009), and are educated in schools which fail to foster critical thinking (Nussbaum 2007).

When we look at this complex interaction closely, we realize that the power emanating from and reified through the use of religious politics, both at the macro- and micro-level, is linked to forms of subjectivity aimed

---

[2]Virat Kohli is an Indian international cricketer and was elected as the captain of the National Cricket Team in India in 2017.

at the training of individual bodies and utilizing their capacities. Adolescents are, therefore, produced as religious subjects through an assemblage of governmental practices, political rationality, and everyday experiences. When Seema and Priya tried to humiliate Razia because of her religious identity, it was a practice of discrimination emanating from a host of power relations operating at school, in homes/families, among communities and embedded in their regimes of knowledge and practices. The formation of a religious subject is, therefore, contingent on both the practices of government and the practices of self.

In order to understand how students identify as religious subjects, the question we must ask is How are students trained, through regimes of knowledge and practice, to conduct others and themselves as religious subjects?

To understand this, let us take draw inferences from our conversations with Hamidbhai, a member of the Muslim community. When we asked him why he doesn't allow Nasreen, his extremely intelligent and extrovert girl, to participate in theater activities we had planned for the students in the school, he said,

> I won't allow my daughter to participate in the drama. Do you want me to be comfortable with her dancing in front of others? Is she an object for display? You know what people will think of her if she dances when we have young boys and old men from the village in the audience? These are all effects of modernization. She has learnt to question me.

Here, Nasreen is constituted as a subject and is taught to internalize certain actions as integral to how she should conduct her body, how she should express her family's belief system in and through her bodily practices, and how she should situate and deploy her body in the presence of other bodies. These regimes of practices influence the way Nasreen talks to others in her class, the way she dresses, the way she behaves in the presence of others, the way she expresses herself, and most importantly the way she thinks. Analyzing these regimes of practices, therefore, includes two steps:

1. We identify the multitudinous elements which constitute the regimes.
2. We examine the processes through which these elements are assembled into coherent forms of institutional practices and how these processes are contingent on particular forms of knowledge through which the goals are realized (Ghatak and Abel 2013).

For instance, Nasreen as a subject is subsumed in the prevailing regime of practices in and through various elements such as family environment, media ecologies, community interactions, education, religious organization, and so on. These elements, however, are not mutually exclusive in that they have developed strong links with and give rise to stable forms of organization. In the case of Nasreen, her entire family visits the mosque along with other members from her community. They have a shared knowledge system which is informed by media narratives, community rules, religious teachings, personal opinions, family belief systems, and so on. Her interactions in school are shaped by these elements and she chooses to spend most of her time with girls from her religious community, i.e., Muslims. Her body is a site inscribed with these institutionalized practices and the school provides her the space to enact this acquired subjectivity.

Regimes of practices is an overarching structure which makes possible "...borrowings across institutions and innovations within them" (Dean 1999). It is supplemented with regimes of truth [knowledge] informed by a dominant rationality and consists of particular forms of knowledge, techniques, mechanisms, instruments, and other technological dimensions through which these practices operate (Stingl 2011; Weir 2008). This involves analyzing "... the types of discourse [society] harbours and causes to function as true, the mechanisms and instances which enable one to distinguish true from false statements, the way in which each is sanctioned, the techniques and procedures which are valorised for obtaining truth, and the status of those who are charged with saying what counts as true" (Foucault 1980). In other words, there can be no regime of practice without a corresponding constitution of a field of knowledge and no knowledge which doesn't necessitate the constitution of a site of practice (1997). This gives rise to a power–knowledge complex formed by a dynamic relation between regimes of practices and regimes of truth–knowledge.

These elements operate at two levels, the macro and the micro, which are delineated in the following sections.

GOVERNING AT THE MACRO-LEVEL

In these villages, religion as a governing formation creates guidelines through which subjects identify and locate their position and that of others in religious communities through three formal agencies/macro-structures of power, i.e., the system of governing (*Panchayat* and village elders), the school, and the media. The dominant forms of rationalities are inscribed in heterogenous systems of practices through which dominant identity of the subject is formed and reified. These rationalities also determine the capacities formed which in turn regulate the conduct of the subject.

System of Governance

In the villages, the political system revolves around religious and caste identities of people contesting for the political posts. People vote for their religion and caste. Manojbhai, a resident who works as a librarian, explained,

> In our village, there are 2879 upper caste Hindus consisting of *Thakore, Parmar, Raval,* and *Desai* and 537 lower caste Hindus including the *Chauhans, Vankars,* and *Vagharis.* On the other hand, there are only 1384 Muslim voters including both the upper and the lower castes; mainly the *Pathans* and the *Saiyed.* During the *Panchayat* elections, therefore, it is very difficult for a Muslim candidate to win because Hindus always vote for a Hindu candidate. Look at the list of people who have been the *Sarpanch* all these years; a Muslim candidate hasn't won the *Panchayat* election in the past 15 years.

Many residents articulate the same opinion. Kallubhai, Ishwarbhai, and Namitaben argue that political affiliations are articulated based on religious identities. The system of governance which emerges from such an arrangement limits characteristic ways in which a [religious] subject sees and is being seen, the distinctive ways in which they think, and act. The ways in which religious subjects learn to conduct themselves include analyzing the mechanisms, techniques, sites, and instruments used to regulate and/or enact their subjectivity. For instance, the elected village committees, through informal rules, ensure that members of one community do not participate in the religious festivals of the other. During Navratri, Muslim adolescents are never encouraged to go to the *garba* grounds to participate in the festivities. Similarly, during *Eid-ul-Milad,*[3] Hindu adolescents never join the Muslim processions or visit the Muslim neighborhood for participating in the celebrations. Manojbhai explains,

> There are unsaid rules; we are very cordial with each other but never participate in one another's religious celebrations. Even during marriages, if you

---

[3] *Eid-ul-Milad* is the observance of the birthday of the Islamic prophet Muhammad which is generally celebrated in the third month of the Islamic calendar.

get an invite from a member of the other community you are supposed to respectfully decline it with an excuse.

This can be taken as an instance where the regime of government establishes the boundaries which limit interactions between different communities. According to the regimes of government, therefore, governance is not simply a means to arrange people into neat pockets for accommodation, to order them, or to help them move around. It involves more than just a process to create a systematic order in the society. Government, here, involves "... some sort of attempt to deliberate on and to direct human conduct" (Dean 1992). The process conceives human conduct as something that can be shaped, controlled, regulated, and turned to eventuate certain ends.

The political system in these villages consists of the elected committees and also some informal groups of powerful village elders who codify rules, laws, and norms for the residents of the village. These norms and rules created and reinforced by the political/governance system in the villages are borrowed by another macro-institution of power, i.e., the primary school. In the next section, we will delineate how the school uses various regulatory techniques and forms of knowledge/practice to regulate the conduct of adolescents, thus encouraging them to operate in accordance with the expectations of the dominant rationality.

The Primary School

In these villages, the regulatory power of religion also operates through educational institutions that work as material sites for constituting the collective psyche and "generating a dominant frame used by adolescents to interpret social realities" (Youdell 2006). In particular, the unapologetic reliance on rote-learning and a banking system of education in which power hierarchies are reified and uncritical submission to authority is considered to be a virtue serves to train young adolescents to reinforce dominant rationalities uncritically and unquestioningly.

When we started working as a media educator, our first challenge was to encourage students to participate in classroom discussions. They were not only apprehensive to ask questions and raise their voice but were often reprimanded and punished by other teachers when they did so. Punishment included harsh forms of disciplining such as slapping, kicking, using a ruler to beat the child, or milder forms such as not allowing them to attend a class, asking them to stand for the entire session, or to write an apology letter for misbehaving. The school follows a regime of practices of punishment to constitute the classroom as governable and administrable.

Let us understand this using an example. During a class, Rajendrabhai, who teaches social science to seventh and eighth grade students, asked Aarish to answer a question related to the constitution of the country. Aarish is a shy student and finds it difficult to answer questions confidently in front of the entire class. He was, therefore, hesitant while answering the question to which Rajendrabhai said, "You can memorize quotes from the Quran but won't ever be able to recite anything from your school textbooks" and slapped him hard. This behavior is problematic at various levels. To begin with, teachers are trained as subjects with authority who have the responsibility of meting out punishment to students when they deem necessary. On the other hand, students are wedged into roles which demand obedience and uncritical acceptance of the authority. This becomes the programmatic rationality of the school. This rationality doesn't exist in and of itself; it is interwoven with an intentionality brought into play by the teachers and students (Dorrestijn 2012).

When the teachers used a remark with a religious slant to insult a student, he brought to the site an intentionality which was guided to specific ends and purposes. The purpose of this teacher was to declare his allegiance to his Hindu community by insulting the religious other, i.e., the Muslim student consequently reinforcing practices of religious discrimination. In other words, when we analyze the regimes of practices and knowledge in the school we realize that religious and caste identities play a role in constructing the intentionalities of teachers and students alike.

The classroom, therefore, becomes a field of dispersed relations that are the conditions of action and discourse. The regimes of practices with their inherent rationalities and intentionalities act as the material site where the regimes of truth are realized and contained. This problematizes a simple distinction between the neutral, technical aspects of regulation in school and their political dimensions. The techniques of power used in the school such as the authority of the teacher, modes of punishment, the seating arrangement of adolescents, interaction between students, and other practices/forms of conduct are polyvalent and can be put to serve different purposes. The way they are used in the school, however, is coherent with particular forms of rationality which, in this case, is the constitution and control of religious subjects.

Our findings substantiate the theoretical argument made by Simons and Masschelein (2011) that schools play an important role in legitimizing certain types of individual and collective identities by delegitimizing alternate forms of identities, realities, and practices. The disciplinary and regulatory powers at work in the school define and limit how students can conduct themselves in relation to the religious other. In the classroom, for instance, students are presented with two choices—sit with the classmates from one's religious community or deny obliging. The classroom is designed as a spatial site where it is difficult for students and teachers to think of alternatives such as sitting according to roll numbers, changing seats every day so that they get to interact with all their classmates, partnering with students who complement their skills and abilities, or with those who help them learn better and so on. In the school, therefore, different modalities of subject formation converge in and are increasingly experienced as a fragment of the religious identity.

In the next section, we analyze media ecologies of adolescents in these villages and draw a trajectory of how media representations act as "a material site and an embodied form" (Leone 2004) for the articulation of religious guidelines.

Media Ecologies and Representations

Media discourses are implicated in the formation of subjects as they shape and influence the utterances, actions, thoughts, and subjectivity of individuals. Media discourse becomes a ritual which is enacted on the basis of the practice of limitations and exclusions—it marks out the boundaries of acceptable and unacceptable, normal and abnormal, sanity, and madness (Foucault 1970).

The local media—both mainstream and community driven and in various formats such as print, video, audio, and WhatsApp messages—define ways in which the religious other is perceived—providing interpretive frameworks that resonate across social space (Bhatia and Pathak-Shelat 2017; Rajagopal 2001). Media discourses, therefore, are not simple representations of the society and a group of signs. They are practices "… that form the objects of which we speak" (Foucault 1972), influencing how ideas are put into actions and how they can be used to regulate conduct. According to Hall (1994), media discourse makes few things acceptable, both in speaking and in action, by ruling out all the other possibilities.

Representation, therefore, is a practice through which an event is constituted, conduct is regulated, and language is controlled. Harishbhai, a senior Hindu resident from these villages who self-identifies as a liberal citizen of the country, reflects on the role of media in perpetuating the religious divide by circulating negative images of the "other." He explains,

> Regional media is no more an independent, justice-seeking institution. They prefer to represent views of the fringe elements from the community who are too eager to give out extreme and rash statements. Also, newspapers such as *Sandesh* and *Gujarat Samachar* and regional TV channels such as TV9 and ABP allot substantial coverage to Hindu religious stories and teachings. They sometimes also include teachings from the Buddhist, Jain, and Christian religions but they never talk about Islam. You should see the supplement in *Gujarat Samachar*, Dharmalok, published every Thursday... This creates resentment in the Muslim youth.

Here, an absence of narratives related to the Muslim community is a kind of discursive silence anchored on the politics of exclusion which limits the scope of engaging with the religious other (Jordan 2015). Foucault uses the term "conditions of possibilities" to understand the reasons behind this formation of a truth, to identify what alternate possibilities the present erased to claim authenticity and to describe ways in which individuals subject themselves to an uncritical acceptance of a religious identity (Foucault 1988). It is in this sense that Foucault writes, "There has been much less study of what has been rejected from our civilization. It [thus] seemed interesting to me to try to understand our society and civilization in terms of its system of exclusion, of rejection, of refusal, in terms of what it does not want, its limits, the way it is obliged to suppress a certain number of things, people, processes, what it must let fall into oblivion, its repression-suppression system" (Foucault 1970). In this light, silence or the act of speaking and verbalization is indeed the act of controlling thoughts by analyzing its potential to lead an individual toward submission and/or subjectification.

What is important to note here is that these media representations demand "acceptance" in lieu of a sense of social security and other advantages gained from membership in a community (Jordan 2015). This involves circulating messages, promoting media narratives which support a particular idea, and initiating discussions to reinforce their religious communities in classrooms and other public spaces. In other words, discourse is circulated through a combination of mediated and non-mediated channels of communication and religion operates as a power system feeding on texts—written, visual, audio, and otherwise—as a means for shaping the lived experience of community members (Banaji 2015).

Many of the residents, for instance, agreed that informal discussions in the public spaces in the village such as the temple grounds, the tea stalls near *Bhagor*, i.e., the main gate of the villages, the area around the mosque, retails shops, and house *verandas* were the most fertile grounds for discussing politics, news, religions, culture, movies, and family affairs. Rajniben, a homemaker, thinks that such informal discussions at public spaces help them understand what their community thinks about issues and ideas. These discussions help them understand the unspoken rules, decipher the accepted code of conduct, and help them weigh their standing in the society.

The importance of community life, reliance on interpersonal interactions, and peer circles and their influence on the opinions and ideas of the residents of these villages depict how the macro-politics plunges into micro-politics and influence residents at an individual level. In the next section, we explain how the dominant rationality of religious politics shape the political reality of the subjects with the help of regulatory techniques and moral arguments; it operates both at the macro-level of governing the population while dovetailing into technologies of discipline that operate at the micro-level.

MICRO-POLITICS AND PRACTICES OF RELIGIOUS DISCRIMINATION

In these villages, micro-politics can be conceptualized as everyday experiences of the adolescents and the residents. Residents identify public spaces as regular sites to enact their subjectivities and articulate their [religious and political] ideas. All the Muslim adolescents, for instance, attend the evening *namaaz* at the mosque. After the namaaz, they take classes in religious studies conducted by a *maulvi*. According to them, the mosque becomes a site where they cultivate new relations, interact with their friends, discuss ideas, and get to learn new concepts. We visited them near the mosque one evening and asked what the *maulvi* had taught them. Aashiyana said,

> He talked about the book from the sky- Quran. He said that the *Allah*, almighty, revealed *Quran* on Prophet Mohammed. It teaches us that there

is one true god who has created the entire world i.e. *Allah Talah*. People, however, follow other lesser gods because they have gone astray. It is our duty to bring them in *Allah talah's* blessed realm.

As shown, adolescents are taught that there is "one true god" and everyone who follows a different religion worships a "lesser god." This reaffirms their faith in the idea that Hindus are inferior, have gone astray, and are morally corrupt. Also, Muslim students enact these differences in the class when they refuse to accommodate Hindu adolescents in group projects.

Once, while we were preparing a schedule for theater classes with seventh grade students, we asked them if they'd be available to stay after the school. Some of the Hindu students suggested to reschedule it the next day as they'd be busy celebrating *Raksha Bandhan*[4] on the day we had suggested. To this, a Muslim student, Sameer, joked, "Ma'am, keep it on August 7. It is not our festival and these *Thakores* [referring to the group of Hindu kids] are of no use at all. Why wait for them." When some of the Hindu students protested, the Muslim adolescents shouted, "Then draw your swords!" and started laughing.

Here, we observe that micro-politics operates at the level where individuals and groups engage with one another (Collier 2009). The practical dispositions of power [micro-politics] can be witnessed in "... characteristic networks, currents, relays, and points of support" (Foucault 1972) which enable individuals to develop, experience, modify, and sustain their subjectivities in the society. For young students, these networks and relations are enabled in and through their engagement with the community. Their families play a crucial role in socializing them within a dominant rationality. When Irfanbhai, a mechanic, proudly declares that there has never been an inter-faith marriage in the village, he brings to light the various forces that function to maintain the sanctity of religious boundaries between the two communities. He elaborates how adolescents from a young age are educated to believe that the Hindus are followers of lesser gods and are sinners because they worship idols. Muslim adolescents should, therefore, steer clear of nurturing familial relationships with them.

---

[4]Raksha Bandhan is a festival celebrated largely by the Hindu community in India where the sister ties a thread around the wrist of her brother; the thread is meant to protect him from misfortune. Most of the Hindu married women in these villages visit the houses of their brothers on Raksha Bandhan to perform the ritual of tying a rakhi and spend time with their parents.

The macro-politics creates a society within which the individuals operate but the micro-politics enable them to conduct the self and others in accordance with the norms, systems, conventions, and codes of this society. The techniques and mechanisms used by individuals to conduct the self and others as subjects (in this case, religious subject) are called the technologies of the self.

Technologies of the self, therefore, have the potential to constitute subjects in the service of the dominant social, political, and cultural rationality, thus reinforcing power hierarchies (Falzon 2013). Yet, technologies of the self also invite active participation on the part of the subject with regard to their relations with themselves and others. This theoretical explication rests within Foucault's conceptualization of power as constitutive rather than simply coercive, enabling subjects to act and not simply limiting their ability to act. Power, thus, is discursive and pervades the entire social field and this pervasiveness means that resistance is not marginal but multiple and active. In certain contexts, individuals can use the same power that is manifest in the social field through technologies of the self to resist, challenge, and/or disrupt dominant rationalities. Technologies of the self provide possibilities for micro-disruptions through a set of counter-practices crafted to challenge the dominant rationality. Because technologies of the self presuppose a conscious, rational, and deliberative action on the part of the religious subjects, many scholars contend that it opens possibilities for subversion and the development of alternate rationalities.

This is done by creating conditions of uncertainty and by critically examining how governmentality operates as a religious order. To develop practices of counter-conduct, we need a site to enact resistance, a site that is within the broader framework of governmentality, serves as a regulatory force for managing the population, and yet penetrates the lives of individuals in ways that can influence a counter micro-politics (Death 2010). Through this research, we identify media education as a site where practices of counter-conduct can be enacted to examine the discourses and practices of religious governmentality, disrupt the normalizing influence of the dominant rationality, and create alternate conditions of being. We propose to use media education to facilitate modes of counter-conduct resistance to create conditions which allow young students to resist and/or subvert power hierarchies in their immediate community environments. The next chapter delineates how critical media education can provide practices of counter-conduct to provoke forms of resistance among religious subjects.

REFERENCES

Ahmed, S. (2010). The role of the media during communal riots in India: A study of the 1984 Sikh riots and the 2002 Gujarat riots. *Media Asia, 37*(2), 103–111.

Banaji, S. (2015). Behind the high-tech fetish: Children, work and media use across classes in India. *The International Communication Gazette, 77*(6), 577–599.

Bhatia, K. (2016). Understanding the role of media education in promoting religious literacy: A critical pedagogy for primary school students in rural India. *Media Education Research Journal, 7*(2), 11–28.

Bhatia, K., & Pathak-Shelat, M. (2017). Media literacy as a pathway to religious literacy in pluralistic democracies: Designing a critical media education pedagogy for primary school children in India. *Interactions: Studies in Communication & Culture, 8*(2), 189–209.

Collier, S. (2009). Typologies of power: Foucault's analysis of political government beyond 'governmentality'. *Theory, Culture and Society, 26*(6), 78–108.

Dean, M. (1992). A genealogy of the government of poverty. *Economy and Society, 21*(3), 215–251.

Dean, M. (1999). *Governmentality: Power and rule in modern society*. London: Sage.

Death, C. (2010). Counter-conducts: A Foucauldian analytics of protest. *Social Movement Studies, 9*(3), 235–251.

Dorrestijn, S. (2012). Technical mediation and subjectivation: Tracing and extending Foucault's philosophy of teaching. *Philosophy & Technology, 25*(2), 221–241.

Falzon, C. (2013). Foucault, subjectivity, and technologies of the self. In Z. Falzon, T. O'leary, & J. Sawicki (Eds.), *A companion to Foucault* (pp. 510–525). New York: Wiley Blackwell.

Foucault, M. (1970). *The order of things: An archaeology of the human sciences*. New York: Pantheon Books.

Foucault, M. (1972). *The archaeology of knowledge* (A. M. Sheridan Smith, Trans.). New York: Pantheon Books.

Foucault, M. (1980). Power/knowldge. In *Selected interviews and other writings 1972–1977*. Brighton: The Harvester Press.

Foucault, M. (1988). Technologies of the self. In L. H. Martin, H. Gutman, & P. H. Hutton (Eds.), *Technologies of the self: A seminar with Michel Foucault* (pp. 16–49). London: Tavistock.

Foucault, M. (1997). *Discipline and punish: The birth of the prison* (A. Sheridan, Trans.). New York: Random House.

Ghatak, S., & Abel, A. (2013). Power/faith: Governmentality, religion, and post-secular societies. *International Journal of Politics, Culture, and Society, 26*(3), 217–235.

Hall, S. (1994). Culture identity and diaspora. In P. William & L. Chrisman (Eds.), *Colonial discourse and post-colonial theory: A reader* (pp. 392–403). New York: Columbia University Press.

Jain, A. (2010). Beaming it live: 24-hour television news, the spectator and the spectacle of the 2002 Gujarat carnage. *South Asian Popular Culture, 8*(2), 163–179.

Jordan, M. (2015). *Convulsing bodies: Religion and resistance in foucault*. Stanford, CA: Stanford University Press.

Leone, M. (2004). *Religious conversion and identity: Semiotic analysis of texts*. New York: Routledge.

Nussbaum, M. (2007). *The clash within: Democracy, religious violence, and India's future*. Cambridge: Harvard University Press.

Rajagopal, A. (2001). *Politics after television: Hindu nationalism and the reshaping of the public in India*. Cambridge: Cambridge University Press.

Sikand, Y. (2008). *Issues in madrasa education in India*. New Delhi: Hope India Publications.

Simons, M., & Masschelein, J. (2011). Governmental, political and pedagogic subjectivation: Foucault with Ranciere. In M. Simon & J. Masschelein (Eds.), *Ranciere, public education and the taming of democracy* (pp. 76–92). Sydney: Philosophy of Education Society of Australia.

Stingl, A. (2011). Truth, knowledge, narratives of selves: An account of the volatility of truth, the power of semantic agency, and time in narratives of the self. *The American Sociologist, 42*(2/3), 207–219.

Sud, N. (2009). Secularism and the Gujarat state: 1960–2005. *Modern Asian Studies, 42*(6), 1251–1281.

Weir, L. (2008). The concept of truth. *The Canadian Journal of Sociology, 33*(2), 367–389.

Youdell, D. (2006). Subjectivation and performative politics: Butler thinking Althusser and Foucault—Intelligibility, agency and the raced-nationed-religioned subjects of education. *British Journal of Sociology of Religion, 27*(4), 511–528.

CHAPTER 4

Media Education as Counter-Conduct: Analyzing Fields of Visibility and Regimes of Knowledge

Abstract In this chapter, we present a counter-conduct framework for Critical Media Literacy with an aim to encourage young people to identify the limits imposed on them through their subjectification and broaden the field of possible actions and relations. We also discuss the two most important dimensions of this framework, i.e., analyzing the fields of visibility and regimes of knowledge, and enlist a number of media education exercise to re-orient students toward their classmates who belong to a different religious community.

Keywords Counter-conduct · Fields of visibility · Cultural mapping · Body mapping · Regimes of knowledge

Introduction: Government and Freedom

According to the analytics of governmentality (Dean 1999), there is a mutually constitutive relationship between government and resistance, power, and freedom. The regimes of thoughts and practices which entail *subjectification* of individuals recognize the one governed as a locus of freedom. In other words, the general axes of government, i.e., its *techne* (power), *epistemes* (truth), and *ethos* (identify) are exercised on free subjects

© The Author(s) 2019
K. V. Bhatia and M. Pathak-Shelat, *Challenging Discriminatory Practices of Religious Socialization among Adolescents*,
https://doi.org/10.1007/978-3-030-29574-5_4

who embody capacities to think and act in various ways and sometimes in ways not anticipated by authorities. Power relations, therefore, are "non-subjective and intentional" (Foucault 1997) which implies that the act of governing is not focused on regulating bodies in and their entirety but on defining, creating, and limiting the field of possible actions in which these bodies are implicated through disciplinary forces. Power relations are non-subjective because they don't target subjects as inert and consenting but deploy them as elements of its articulation and as incidental to the reification of power relations for particular needs (Heller 1996). These particular needs and not the subjects, according to Foucault, are the real intentions of power relations.

Analyzing resistance in Foucault, therefore, requires re-conceptualizing power relations in order to examine how authorities attempt to regulate and modify actions of subjects so that the particular needs and intentions of a programmatic rationality at play can be realized. This creates an interesting opening for scholars who are interested in examining how individuals are implicated in power relations which are supra-individually imposed while at the same time exercise their capacities of thinking and doing within this self-sustaining power complex in order to govern the conduct of others and the self.

One of the inferences of this proposition when individuals have the freedom to dispense their capacities toward conducting others and themselves according to the dominant rationalities, they also have the freedom to conduct or be conducted in an autonomous way—a freedom to refuse to operate from within the limits of the field of actions devised by authorities (Lorenzini 2016).

This proposition presents a productive rupture in the conceptualization of power as coercive because it reiterates the potency of this "free will." In other words, the "I want to be conducted" is replete with the force of "I want" and so there is a possibility of a transformative shift from "I want" to "I do not want anymore."

How should we understand this refusal to conduct and be conducted? How can the *will to resist* in an individual be theorized and activated? In his work *Security, Territory, Population* (2007), Foucault coins the term counter-conduct in order to designate modes of resistance that operate against "*involute*" rationalities and *technes* of conduct by opposing various power locales instead of villainizing just the state apparatus. This means that counter-conduct is envisaged and practiced from within the interiority of dominant rationalities; instead of rejecting the government, it problematizes modes of conduct perpetuated by the technologies of discipline.

Counter-conduct is defined as "a will not to be governed thusly, like that, by these people, at this price" (1997). Counter-conduct suggests a major re-orientation in the field of actions as it problematizes the process of subjectification and negotiates with the possibility of deploying alternate mechanisms of conduct which transform situations of power. The resistance through counter-conduct is not embedded in a simple refusal of power but in the performance of "alterity" and in enactment of alternate forms of practices of self. It should thus be established that counter-conduct is not a passive underside of power (Davidson 2011); it is performative in that it represents the exercise of will in order to experience possibilities previously inaccessible from within the normalized field of action.

When concepts such as conduct and counter-conduct are mobilized to suggest the practice of will and active intervention by individuals in political and ethical practices that shape us, the force of agency and resistance in Foucault's work becomes visible. This agency is manifest in practices of conduct that are in accordance with the dominant rationality as much as in practices of resistance that create friction in the taken-for-granted assumptions about the present. Counter-conduct, then, shares a theoretical space with the Kantian question "Who we are at this precise moment of history?" (Foucault 1982) as it initiates a new interrogation of the ontology of ourselves and our present in order to allow opportunities where "one can refuse who one is" to become someone else. Foucault explains,

> Probably the principal objective today is not to discover but to refuse what we are. We have to promote new forms of subjectivity while refusing the type of individuality that has been imposed on us for several centuries.

In order to allow for new subjectivities to emerge, individuals must recognize the arbitrariness of rituals and systems that shape our conventional conduct. Counter-conduct is a mode for transcendence from obedience in a known realm into experimentation with subjectivities in the unknown. It is built on the process of subversion—*the techne, epistemes, and ethics* of governmentality are exhibited to invite critical questioning, which might lead to the weakening of explicit modes of conduct (Sokhi-Bulley 2016).

According to Foucault, though shift in subjectives is originary to individuals and experienced from within, we propose that individuals can change situations of power and fields of action in which the existing limits to subjectification are postulated as truth. This can help make intelligible a wide variety of "alternate" ways in which it is possible for the governed to conduct themselves/others and/or be conducted. To create situations conducive for recognizing the need to experiment with alternative subjectivities and to enact practices of counter-conduct in order to experience what a shift in the process of subjectification entails for individuals, we need a site to ideate, enact, and participate in resistance. In this book, we identify critical media education (CML) as a site where counter-conduct can be enacted to examine the discourses and practices of religious governmentality. It is used as a site to reconfigure the fields of visibility, disrupt the normalizing influence of the dominant rationality, and create alternate conditions of being.

CRITICAL MEDIA EDUCATION AS COUNTER-CONDUCT

CML is a set of competencies which enables individuals to read into texts and practices that represent the very fabric of our everyday world. Though media literacy, in general, has focused on developing a mode of analysis and a way of engaging discursively with media texts, in this book we propose that media education as a site can be deployed to encourage individuals to perform their identities (read, alternate subjectivities) and through this act create a fraying in their everyday experiences that are guided by the dominant rationality. CML, therefore, is conceptualized as a performative project where individuals not only articulate but also act their subjectivities and take cognizance of the unintended consequences that such performances have. CML is used as a site to help individuals resolve the disjuncture between their actions' intention and its actual effect (Hoechsmann and Poyntz 2012). CML argues that the act of participating is emblematic of any practice of transformation and operates from within the contours of lived experiences and processes of subject formation.

CML provides a means to open up these experiences and help individuals to act in the world and engage with differences which brings urgency to their transformation. CML is counter-conduct in that it is non-subjective but intentional. It is non-subjective insofar as it shifts its emphasis on the practical materializations of alternate subjectivities and intentional in that it compels individuals to consider the ramifications of their everyday actions.

Young students can't experience this alterity automatically or easily and without adult guidance. One major reason for this is that people are socialized and trained to conform to what is customary, conventional, and naturalized. This is because having opinions which represent nonconformity are neither taught nor encouraged, thus making unconventional behavior a reproach. In order to preserve a pluralist culture where politics of individual differences are valued, we require a means to disrupt this uniformity of conduct.

CML provides a means to challenge this uniformity of conduct by broadening "the limited spectrum of the relational world created and managed by the institutional frameworks of our society" (Davidson 2011). In order to conceive of CML as counter-conduct rooted in the political and ethical axes of equality, we draw on the vision of various other scholars such as Freire (1970, 1973), Giroux (2001), and Arendt (1958) who emphasize on the need to infuse the social fabric in democracies with multiplicity of conducts and rationalities. CML helps study routine behaviors in relation to the larger power complex at play to counter a kind of oblivion inherent in the practice of a dominant rationality, a single narrative, and normalized disciplinary mechanisms. It is the presence of multiple locales, individuals, and practices that sustains a conversation between different people and the "worldliness of the world" (Silverstone 2007).

CML can be used for counter-conduct because it creates a dialectical space wherein competing discourses and conflicting practices converge to inform one another and counteract thoughtlessness (Bennett 2008). It acts as a pivot point between the mode of analyzing and the mode of doing, i.e., it not only gives students opportunities to situate themselves in the wider domain of power relations but also activates in them the need to express their stake in the public culture by appropriating and altering it (Buckingham 2003). It positions students as actors in the world and affords them competencies and opportunities to distance themselves from their uncritical subjective identities and parse the processes through which they were implicated as subjects of religious politics.

According to Foucault (1997), the critical ethos of such a project must be conceived as "... an attitude, [...] a philosophical life in which the critique of what we are is at one and the same time the [...] analysis of the limits that are imposed on us and an experiment with the possibility of going beyond them." This act of "going beyond" and creating ruptures is marked by the mental, physical, and emotional involvement of students who create and immerse themselves in new power situations. The possibility to change situations/relations of powers is dependent on students withdrawing their consent for being conducted in a particular way. In order to exercise this counter-will, in order to express differently, students need technical and analytical competencies along with a site where this resistance can be enacted. Within the theoretical framework of CML, media production is seen as the site for praxis where creative self-expression based on diverse conversations and experiences can materialize (Soep 2006). CML uses all the affordances of representation and creation available in mediated cultures to challenge and/or upend power hierarchies authorized in and through media narratives. If media texts are seen as one of the many mechanisms for conducting individuals, then CML is the counter-conduct that appropriates a series of elements from within these media environments that are reused, re-implanted, reinserted, and taken up to redirect alternative modes of conduct. Producing alternative narratives, therefore, is not the objective of counter-conduct. Media production is the means to resistance that creates a space for individuals from different regimes of truth to come together, converse, analyze, and perform.

In this research, we use CML as counter-conduct and develop a framework, a four-step process, to help students in the *primary school* engage with and question their field of actions and subjectivities. In order to develop this framework, we borrow from Mitchell Dean's "analytics of government" approach (1999). According to this framework, any prevailing situation of power relations and/or governance [of the self and others][1] have four core dimensions that can be appropriated for devising ways to practice counter-conduct and subversion of authority. The first dimension/process involves an analysis of *the field of visibility* the governing authority creates and the ends to which it aims. The second dimension of this framework is the analysis of *the regimes of knowledge* which refers to the ways in which a space, an individual, a phenomenon, or a belief is converted into an object of inquiry and, in the process, made a part of a dominant system of political rationality.

---

[1] It is important to note here that according to the "analytics of governmentality", the state apparatus often, referred to as the government in common parlance, is just one dimension informing the creation of the dominant rationality. As discussed in Chapter 2, governmentality is the dominant power–knowledge structures constituting of the regimes of practice and truth [knowledge]. It consists of the *techne*, *epistemes*, and *ethos*, all of which constitute and reinforce the dominant rationality. The government is one of the many macro-institutions through which the dominant rationality [of religious discrimination] is disseminated, reinforced, and reified.

The third dimension involves *employing technologies of counter-conduct* in order to practice resistance, i.e., to invoke and create particular practices, techniques, and strategies and a demand to be heard and included (Dean 1999). Finally, the fourth and ultimate step in this process is *accounting for experiences* that students go through when and if they encounter a friction in their subjectivities and fraying around the edges of the dominant rationality. Table 4.1 explains how the framework was adapted for the present work.

In this chapter, we elaborate on and analyze the first two dimensions of the framework, i.e., the fields of visibility and the regimes of

Table 4.1   Critical media education

Counter-conduct framework

Analyzing the fields of visibility: Unpacking ways in which the conduct of religious subjects is influenced and shaped by the predetermined nature of the spaces (physical sites) it inhabits. Analyzing and changing the ways in which religiously exclusive spaces are perceived and used by inserting these sites with differences and the critical presence of the religious other can challenge the dominant forms of thinking and practice

Analyzing the regimes of knowledge: Examining how media representations of the religious other are created and what consequences biased representations can have on the stake of a given community in the society can help students be more critical and sensitive while producing content. It is important that students understand how operating from within the regimes of knowledge dominant in their community may lead them to develop ill-informed narratives about the religious other. Students must be encouraged to work in inter-faith teams, collaborate, and negotiate in order to create sensitive and inclusive media narratives

Developing a techne of self: Under this dimension of the framework, students are encouraged to develop practices, mechanisms, and techniques to conduct themselves critically, especially in relation to their interactions with the religious other. They must be equipped with critical skills required to analyze how their religious socialization provide them with a predetermined interpretive frame that influences their perception of the religious other. They can develop critical practices of engagement that allow them to add to their interpretive frames new meanings related to the religious other based on their personal experiences of participating in meaningful conversations with their classmates

Experiencing a friction in subjectivities: Under this dimension, students explore [and enact] their renewed understanding of the religious other in order to redefine their identity as religious subjects. They participate in pedagogic exercises designed to help them conceive of and enact alternate subjectivities, especially with regard to exploring possibilities of collaborating, co-existing, and accepting the religious other. It also involves encouraging students to develop new forms of conduct that allow them to understand and empathize with the lived experiences of the religious other—from beyond their own regimes of knowledge and practice

---

truth/knowledge. We also delineate the CML exercises developed to practice counter-conduct under each dimension and the intended/unintended
consequences of using this framework.

Resisting Conformity Through Critical Media Education

The CML framework we have developed for counter-conduct employs
media culture—embedded in the everyday realities of individuals—as a site
of resistance. According to several scholars (Buckingham and Sefton-Green
2003; Sefton-Green 2006; Willet 2008), this process of examining media
narratives as a constitutive element of the larger cultural contexts allows
researchers and educators to engage in a form of conceptual innovation
marked with a skepticism toward meaning systems, behaviors, conduct,
and experiences that are routinized. It invites individuals to acknowledge
how governmentality operates through the exercise of their will and conduct of their bodies allowing them to repurpose media technologies, texts,
and practices for resistance. In this way, conduct is located in the exercise of
will that is transposed onto the bodies and how they are conducted, regulated, and managed. The supra-individually structured dominant rationality
regulates the manifestation of this will in the forms of behavior individuals
indulge in. The dominant rationality allows for certain discursive horizons
or vistas to be visible, and this opens possibilities for thinking and action
only within selected domains of experiences. It is, therefore, very crucial
for young students to identify the limits imposed on them through their
subjectification and broaden the field of possible actions and relations.

Let us take the example of Shamin, a sixth grade Muslim student, who
has been socialized to believe that Hinduism is the religion of lesser humans,
of those who have fallen prey to the ill-intentions of *saitan*.[2] He identi-
fies himself as a proud Muslim who maintains the sanctity of his religious
identity by acts of compliance such as reading *namaz* five times a day,
avoiding contact with Hindu classmates, and engaging in community service activities coordinated by elders. For him, the only field of action from
which to operate lies in complying with the naturalized definition of "an
ideal Muslim" in his culture. Also, the spectrum of his relational world is

---

[2] *Saitan* is a common word of Arabic origin used to refer to an evil spirit, mainly Satan,
in the Muslim communities. It is sometimes used to refer to an evilly disposed, vicious, or
cunning person/animal.

restricted to individuals/classmates from within his religious community, who inhabit the same regime of truth. How can CML help him identify his subjectification as a process through which the disciplinary forces of governmentality have restricted his relational world as well as his field of action? How can CML help him identify the limits of his subjectivity and open up "... the possibility of an action to accept or reject [these limits] ... to show their contingent nature, or to add up the costs of transgressing them" (Dean 1999)? This is where the first step of the counter-conduct framework comes into play.

Analyzing *fields of visibility* or how the "government [authority] renders visible the space over which government is to be exercised" (Rose 1999) refers to the process of politicizing sites considered apolitical and increasing the visibility of the power relations that guide the construction, meaning, and use of that site. In the next section, we delineate how critical media literacy can enable students to analyze the fields of visibility they inhabit and reify, and devise strategies for counter-conduct to alter the nature of a space by creating friction in its visual constitution.

ANALYZING FIELDS OF VISIBILITY

CML provides the required resources such as technical competencies to create, circulate, and debate new ideas challenging the status quo, material means to produce forms of resistance through critical questioning of the synthetic history, and a site for gaining and aligning public support for new realities. Let us examine the case of Ruchita, a class seventh Hindu student, who refuses to befriend her Muslim classmate Shaziya because she lives in neighborhoods where Hindu children are not welcomed. She explains,

> It becomes difficult to be friends with someone who refuses to meet you after school hours. She lives in the Nano Momin Nivas, a Muslim neighbourhood. I am not allowed to visit her house in the evening because all the village lanes in that area are crowded by Muslim men, dressed in their white *kurtas* and prayer caps. Also, it is an unsaid rule—it is their area.

Like Ruchita, most students from both the communities in the village have preconceived notions about the religious other and the places they inhabit. These places are characterized by cultural markers which are construed as dangerous and harmful. The meaning frames utilized for interpreting the nature of these spaces and consequently engaging with them and the individuals who inhabit these places are borrowed from the repertoire of religious politics circulated in and through various systems of disciplinary governance such as the schools, local communities, and media.

Also, the media representations of spaces that Muslims and Hindus can occupy, for instance, have strengthened a sense of suspicion among the residents of Gujarat. In these villages, public spaces are classified for use either by the Hindu or by the Muslim community. The local media reinforces these segregations by identifying spaces based on the cultural markers they carry, i.e., a mosque, women in *burkhas*, the sound of the azaan, men wearing *namaaz* caps, and so on (Kirmani 2008). Extending these arguments further, we wish to draw attention to the way in which these spaces carry forms of religious dominance and are conducted based on strict Panchayat guidelines regulating the use of these spaces for various community functions. This strategy of creating exclusive spaces for either community has detrimental effects on the psyche of young individuals.

According to several theorists such as Arendt (1978), Giddens (1984), Bakhtin (1981), and Freire (1973), however, the democratic culture of any society can be nurtured only when there is a space where individuals can enter a conversational realm to experience, examine, and engage with the subjectivities introduced by the other. This means that students must be encouraged to re-examine and re-experience these spaces together, as teammates; they must learn to borrow from meaning frames used by different individuals as they juxtapose the weight of their religious identities with the expectations embedded in the unfolding of other students' subjectivities.

This can be made possible only if friction is created in the field of action and the relational spectrum dominant in the village communities. These fields of "becoming [the self]" and "being [in the world in relation to others]" are influenced by force relations that structure the conduct of students as religious subjects. Force can be defined as any factor in a relation that affects the elements embedded in a relationship. Any element that influences the relation between individuals, their experiences, and interactions, with other individuals or institutions, structure the possible field of actions (Davidson 2011). In the case of Ruchita, for instance, her religious identity, the socialization she receives at home, media narratives she consumes, and the interpretive frames she uses to make sense of the world through these narratives define her relationship with her Muslim classmates. When and if she realizes the influence of these elements on how she comes to experience and engage with others, it is likely to allow her to imagine a sense of belonging to an altered reality wherein new relations can emerge.

Once students are aware of these force relations, it becomes possible to modify the field of action by articulating an alternate notion of conduct using media as a material channel.

Here, CML is used as a tactical intervention to situate power in policies and systems of governance that call for a change and then to use this privileged position, a position of awareness, to disrupt the field of visibility by creating a new order of action from within the system. In order to change the existing nature of these spaces in the villages and reinsert these with new meanings based on inter-faith dialogues and experiences shared by students, we used culture mapping, critical presence, and body maps as a counter-conduct CML exercises. We identify three important sites wherein the dominant modes of conduct and thinking are reinforced and reified:

a. Public spaces such as the streets, village lanes, open areas for public use, play areas, and others are sites wherein the dominant rationality is reinforced by regulating ways in which individuals interact with, experience, and conduct [themselves and others] in these spaces.

b. Personal spaces such as courtyards of the houses, neighborhoods, living rooms where family members gather are deployed as sites to formulate codes of conduct regulating the behavior of religious subjects. These codes of conduct influence who can occupy or enter these sites, the kinds of discourses emerging from within these spaces, the meaning-making frames selected to make sense of the world, and the relations [of authority and submission] among people inhabiting these sites.

c. Educational spaces, especially classrooms, have been identified as one of the most important sites where the conduct of religious subjects [students] is validated and practiced. Students enter their classrooms as religious subjects and use this site to enact their religious subjectivities often in the form of practicing discrimination against their classmates from a different religious community [and caste].

In the next section, we describe how the practice of CML exercises such as culture mapping—taking photo-walks to occupying public sites differently, critical presence, and reading in personal sites regulated by the dominant rationality—and body maps to understand how individuals are implicated in the process of reinforcing the dominant rationality can alter the inter-faith relations among students in the villages.

Reimagining Public Spaces Through Counter-Cultural Mapping

A critical use of media can help students create alternate maps for these places, i.e., a cultural representation of spaces which is embedded in experiences of collaborative teamwork and thus in tension with the dominant rationality. Cultural mapping as a counter-conduct CML exercise allows students to combine "the dialectics of practice and analysis" (Buckingham 2003). Encouraging young adolescents to use media, to access new technologies, and to attend to their ethical responsibility as critical actors in their communities begins with identifying pedagogic interventions which combine the analysis of government and society with creative practices of change, contestation, and resistance.

Critical media literacy affords young students with the opportunity to study their immediate community spaces, identify their role in reinvigorating these spaces with politico-religious significance through their activities, and analyze the role of communication channels in reinstating the dominant claims on these spaces by members of their communities. Using CML for remapping the community spaces for greater inclusion is an exercise to understand how power is organized within definite forms of time-space.

In order to help students analyze the existing fields of visibility in their village, it was essential for them to occupy these spaces, and identify different ways of visualizing the fields to be governed. In other words, conditions were created to compel students to picture/imagine who and what was governed and how relations of power and conduct are constituted in a space. For this, we decided to organize photo-walks, four times every week for two months. Classes were divided in teams of six students based on a lottery system. This ensured that both religions had unbiased representation in the teams thus formed. Each class was divided into six teams and each team was taken for a photo-walk twice.

Prior to these photo-walks, a week-long workshop was conducted with students, teaching them the basic competencies of using a mobile camera as well as a DSLR for clicking photos. They were introduced to the technical dimensions of photography such as the focal length of the camera, the shutter speed, zooming and concepts such as over-exposed/under-exposed photos, types of light such as hard light, fill flash, soft and diffused light, and so on. Following this training in technical competencies, we began our photo-walks.

Reimagining Through Photo-Walks

At the outset, the six-member teams were asked to submit a map of the part of the village they wished to visit and document and explain the reasons behind the choices they made. This created problems because Hindu children refused to visit areas in the Muslim neighborhoods and vice versa. Four grade sixth students—Tanisha, Rohan, Ravi, and Rakesh—refused to participate in this activity because their parents had not given them the permission to visit Muslim neighborhoods in the village. Many other students requested that groups be formed on the basis of religious identities so that such differences could be avoided. What was explicit in these reasons, however, was the deep-seated disgust one community had toward the other. Bhavna explained,

> Ma'am, our parents have instructed us not to visit the Muslim neighbourhoods. They are not safe and we don't know why but we feel it.

When I asked her why she insists that the places are unsafe for them, she said,

> How would you feel when you see scary Islamic symbols everywhere? Also, they dress differently. When we go to that area and we don't cover our heads, they stare at us. It is not us always; even they don't like us entering their lanes.

Borrowing from the Foucauldian concept of Bentham's Panopticon, we argue that the presence of these markers locates individual bodies within these spaces in accordance with the modalities of their religious identities (Image 4.1). Practices such as staring at the religious other, asking questions such as "What brings you here," and reprimanding young children of the other community from utilizing spaces represent the omnipresent surveillance of religious politics. Cultural mapping as a pedagogic exercise in media literacy makes visible the techniques of surveillance operating in and through the material organization of conduct. Media can be employed as a site to disturb such permanent and predetermined visibility in these spaces that regulate the behavior of village residents, especially young students. It can be used to encourage students to create counter-maps, a technique within the field of cultural mapping, to challenge the village's formal description of these spaces, to appropriate effective and official techniques of representation, and to create a different narrative.

Image 4.1   This photo was clicked by Nausreen, an eighth grade Muslim student, during a photo-walk. According to her, "This picture depicts the core of our lives. Our God is everywhere—on streets, in our houses, and in our behaviour"

During the photo-walks, therefore, teams of students who were allowed by their parents to participate in this activity visited different areas of the village together. They were asked to click photos of these spaces that were exclusive to particular religious communities and create stories around it. Though students were asked to work as a team while clicking photos, each of them was expected to submit a personal narrative related to the place. Some of the teams used framing as a technique to weave beautiful narratives related to what those spaces meant in their routines. For instance, a team of students from the eighth grade decided to photograph the open grounds that are covered with Banyan trees near the *Ambaji* temple. While selecting the place, Muslim students expressed discomfort because they didn't visit these grounds very frequently (Image 4.2).

As mentioned earlier, these grounds are marked by the presence of a huge temple and are considered to be "off limits" for Muslim adolescents. Hindu students, however, were very excited to visit those grounds and

Image 4.2   Open grounds with Banyan trees near the Ambaji temple: This photo was clicked by an eighth grade student, Kamlesh, and submitted as a personal narrative. According to him, "The Banyan tree stands for growth and survival. It provides protection to the [Hindu] devotees and promises them sustenance"

swing on the roots of the trees. They decided to convince their teammates and reflected on how much fun it would be to swing on the Banyan trees.

What was particularly evident from such instances is that when students are encouraged to work as teammates, it brings to light new forms of affective intensities—removed from established forms of conduct, naturalized codes, and routinized behavioral patterns (Amin 2010; Foucault 1997). The development of these new forms of affective intensities is a center for counter-conduct because it introduces the "ethics of care" (Held 2002; Hutchings 2002) where there should be rules and habits. This theory of "ethics of care" presupposes a concern for the self and the other, "... especially those who are dependent and vulnerable" (Pathak-Shelat 2014). This is manifest in forms of acting, conversing, and engaging with others through media technologies and platforms.

As the Hindu students succeeded in convincing their Muslim co-workers, the team decided to visit the open grounds and document their experiences through photography. As they walked these streets together, they were seen discussing important details regarding framing and editing, creating a cultural disruption in the order of things in the Hindu neighborhood. Muslim students were recognized as teammates and given the respect they deserved. Hindu students took the lead to make their Muslim teammates more comfortable with the surrounding, introducing them to their neighbors, their relatives, and friends and also helping them understand the meaning of various cultural practices witnessed on the roads. As Hindus and Muslims occupied the streets together, they created for the residents of the village a visual spectacle and a language of analysis that was no longer dependent on the preconceived image of those spaces. This act of occupying places was an act of visual defiance against religious politics—a discriminatory ideology which creates an endless fear of "being seen" in a particular place (Malmvig 2016). In their roles as the authors of these narratives and with access to media technologies, students asserted their identity as a political subject in their societies.

Though their individual photo narratives were highly influenced by their religious identities, when they were asked to submit a joint narrative, they invited multiple perspectives from their teammates and often initiated discussions related to production decisions and the socio-political implications of these narratives on their social positioning as religious subjects. For instance, while discussing how to best depict the importance of a Banyan tree in the lives of children, Muslim and Hindu students had different narratives and wanted to use different points of reference and framing techniques. Hindu students wanted to portray it as a pious site and have a temple in the frame. On the other hand, Muslim students felt that such a narrative would leave no room for them to contribute as they were not familiar with the Hindu culture and traditions. After a prolonged discussion, two girls from the team suggested that they develop a photo-story related to a theme which runs common in the lives of all the teammates. They, thus, decided to rearticulate the space as a playground through their photo-story and discuss the different ways in which the Banyan tree could be used for entertainment and leisure purposes (Images 4.3 and 4.4).

If we compare the earlier photo of the banyan tree with the one in this story, we see a significant change. The earlier photo was submitted by Kamlesh, a Hindu student, as a personal narrative and included the temple in the frame. The photo in this story, however, is marked by the presence of Muslim girl students, standing in front of the tree, occupying this space, and changing its definition through their presence.

Image 4.3 Expansive: The banyan tree is large and strong. It teaches us to provide shade to everyone by taking all, small and big, under its cover

It is, however, crucial to acknowledge here that the narratives students created in teams were not always expressed in their authentic voices. In other words, working in groups, under the guidance of a media educator, can sometimes pressurize them to produce flat and generic storytelling (Buckingham et al. 2003) or narratives that are socially acceptable to the classroom community. Soep (2006), however, uses Bakhtin's notion of "double-voiced discourse" (1981) to explicate how creative practices can help locate students in a dialogic relation with others. Bakhtin uses this notion of the "double-voiced discourse" to argue that while expressing and asserting their own identities through content production, young people weave others' voices in their utterances and give rise to "... an intertextual form of speaking woven through a mixing together of one's own words with the words of others" (Soep 2006). This suggests that narratives thus produced are profoundly social—they reflect the material and ideological world young students inhabit. In that, even if they produce narratives that are not true to their regimes of truth and practices, the emergence of concepts intrinsic to the "ethics of care" such as acceptance, empathy, love, and

Image 4.4   No Boundaries: Like the huge Banyan tree, we will be expansive. We will love and play together. We will not let our caste, language, and religion divide us. We will spread happiness by playing together

respect reveals that these experiences are available in their environments and if given the right opportunities they can engage with them.

For instance, a group of seventh grade students selected courtyards of their houses as spaces to be reclaimed from the restrictions imposed on "who is invited and who can visit." They wanted to document the court-yards of all the team members and identify ways in which the space invited conversations. According to Rijwan,

> These open spaces just outside our houses are regulated by the codes created by our parents. For instance, when it is time for *namaaz* my mother would beat me up if I were to stand in the courtyard talking to someone. Also, my father's friends often come over to visit him on Saturdays and they sit in the courtyard to have tea. Children and women are not allowed when the men are having discussions about politics. We are not allowed to participate or question. And if I invite some of my Hindu classmates and socialize with them just for the sake of fun and leisure, my mother won't approve of it. It is not as if we don't have Hindu people visiting us; but they do it only if there is something urgent and important.

This gave us ideas on how the courtyards could be appropriated for two things. First, students wanted to emphasize that engagement between Hindus and Muslims is not always for selfish motives. Engaging with the other, sharing the same space with them, and learning to be comfortable in each other's presence are important ways of disrupting the normalized order of things. Second, occupying these spaces that are beyond the reach of students was their way of asserting their role as political subjects who had an equal stake in the meaning-making mechanisms of the villages. The latter proposition was put forth especially by girl students who had been systematically removed from political/public discussions and felt the need to displace adult formulated codes of conduct as vital nodes of their identities and find ways to express themselves.

Reimagining Personal Spaces Through Critical Presence and Thinking

Besides the public spaces, students were keen to change the rules and codes of conduct related to their engagement in and with personal spaces such as courtyards of their houses. We, thus, created another CML exercise designed to populate personal spaces with differences in conduct, thinking, and presence. We decided to appropriate the courtyards of houses in the villages and invite students to occupy these spaces which are strictly regulated by codes of conduct—who can visit, when, and why. We inserted the strictly regulated personal spaces with the critical presence of the religious other and created conditions where both Hindus and Muslims were encouraged to engage in a collective meaning-making process. They were compelled, in a way, to share a space and collaborate to make sense of media narratives. Students regardless of their religious identities were encouraged to participate in the "critical thinking sessions" organized in house courtyards, sometimes in the Hindu neighborhoods and at the other times in the Muslim neighborhoods.

In this CML exercise, several student groups decided to hold newspaper reading sessions in the courtyards of their houses and invited all their classmates to participate in this activity. In order to change the composition of their courtyards, it was important to situate "defiant bodies" in its otherwise stable structure and acknowledge their presence. This phenomenon is defined as "inserting regulated spaces [here, personal sites] with the critical presence of the religious other."

We designed a CML exercise titled "*Samachar nu arthghatan*" (Interpreting the news) and for two days different students identified stories they wanted to read to the class. Each student who volunteered was given 5 minutes to read the news in the courtyard followed by 10 minutes of discussion where their classmates tried to analyze the texts based on three simple parameters: who wrote the text, for what reason, and who is the intended audience.

Students selected very interesting texts that revealed the biases of regional newspapers against one or the other religious community. Though most of the narratives discussed politics in Gujarat and how it was represented through newspapers, two of them could be categorized as narratives that dealt with "religious politics" and created critical discussion. Let us look at one of these examples (Image 4.5).

The student who presented a reading of this narrative argued that Muslims should cooperate with Hindus and respect their religious beliefs. Ruksaar, a seventh grade Muslim student, however, remarked,

> They put a ban on the consumption of even non-vegetarian food during the Jain festival. That is not right. Each religion should celebrate their food habits without being forced to follow other people's lifestyle and call it as 'respecting the other'.

Image 4.5 Headline: To prevent cow slaughter, a congregation of Muslims will be organized in Chikhali (Place: Navsari. Date: June 17, 2016. The cow protection committees of the Muslim society in Navsari and Mahuva taluka have organized a congregation on June 21, 2016 to discuss how to prevent cow slaughter. The Ulma of the taluka, Mufti Harun Nadvi Sahab, along with the Chief Maulana, Fayyaz Laturi, have come together to be a part of this)

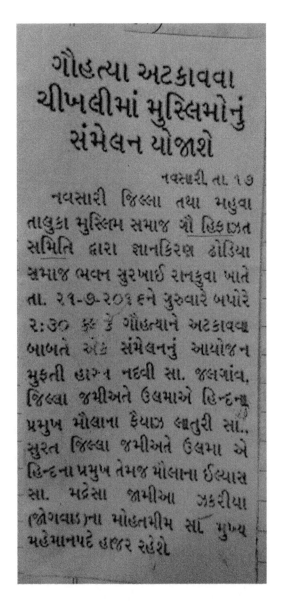

This statement created immense discomfort in the courtyard for two reasons. First, Hindu students felt alienated because they were in the courtyard of a Muslim classmate and were surrounded by Muslim families and friends. Ruksaar felt very confident because it was a space owned by the people of her community. The Hindu students, on the other hand, were scared to critically engage with this statement. Karan, a Hindu student, finally mustered courage to contest this and said, "But who told you that all Hindus are vegetarian. When they impose bans on the consumption of non-vegetarian food, they are also restricting food choices of Hindu people. Let us, therefore, not look at this from the perspective of a Hindu-Muslim debate. It is more about our fundamental rights as citizens of this country." This statement was truly fascinating for it brought to light a possibility of investigating new relations, i.e., relations between individuals as political subjects and not as religious bodies, that were very different from the ones proposed to us in our society. According to Foucault (2007), any form of counter-conduct, be it dialogic or practice-based, can change modes of existence by inventing new modalities of relations. The real effects of the struggle for rights should be imagined in terms of a change in schemes of behavior and how individuals relate to the self in relations to the others. This is what happened when the same group of students visited a Hindu classmate's courtyard and were presented with the following narrative (Image 4.6).

When a Hindu student read this in the courtyard of a Hindu student Rutvi's house, all the Muslim students showed signs of discomfort. They didn't know how to ask questions. Adding to this was the presence of a school teacher and Rutvi's parents in the courtyard listening attentively to what was being said. One Hindu student, Manhar, turned toward me and asked, "Why is the headline constructed as a question? Are they not sure yet that these things have been announced by politicians?" Before I could answer, Rutvi's grandfather decided to intervene, "Well, the fact of the matter is that Ayodhya is the birthplace of Ram. If they wish to win the elections they will have to please their voters." Manhar, however, was not convinced. He continued,

> If this has already been selected as an agenda, why does the newspaper not say so? There is indecisiveness in the way it is written. This can mean two things—either they don't want to take the responsibility of dealing with this issue critically or they are not sure themselves.

Many students joined the discussion and had different things to say. The newspaper reading session created friction in the courtyard of this Hindu household that had till late welcomed only narratives that supported their

રામમંદિરના નામે યુપી ચૂંટણી જીતવા વ્યૂહ, સાળંગપુરમાં અમિત શાહે સોગઠાં ગોઠવ્યાં?

રામમંદિરનું બાંધકામ શરૂ કરવાનો હીડન એજન્ડા હવે અમલમાં મૂકાઈ રહ્યો છે?

■કેટલાંક સાધુઓની હાજરી અને નેતાઓનાં લાંબા સેકાણથી રાજકીય ગરમાવો

ગાંધીનગર, તા.૮

ઉત્તર પ્રદેશ વિધાનસભાની માર્ચ ૨૦૧૭માં આવી રહેલી ચૂંટણીના સંદર્ભે ભાજપના રાષ્ટ્રીય પ્રમુખ અમિત શાહે સોમવારે નિવેદન કર્યું હતું કે, ઉત્તર પ્રદેશની ચૂંટણીમાં અયોધ્યામાં રામમંદિર બનાવવાનો મુદ્દો એજન્ડા પર હશે. આ નિવેદન બાદ તુરંત તેઓ ગુજરાત આવ્યા છે અને ગુજરાતનું ધાર્મિક સ્થળ સાળંગપુર હનુમાન મંદિર ખાતે તેઓ લાંબુ રોકાણ કરીને કેટલાંક સંતો સાથે ચર્ચા કરી રહ્યા છે. રાજકીય વર્તુળો કહે છે કે, અહીં કેટલાંક સંતો સાથે રામમંદિર અંગે શું કરવું જોઈએ તે અંગે હીડન એજન્ડા સાથે સંતો સાથે ચર્ચા કરીને આગામી રણનીતિ નક્કી કરે તેવી સંભાવના છે.

સાધુઓની હાજરી અને નેતાઓના લાંબા રોકાણથી રાજકીય ગરમ માહોલ ઊભો થયો છે. સાળંગપુર ખાતે સ્વામિનારાયણ સંપ્રદાયના ૭૦૦ જેટલાં સંતોની એક શિબિર ચાલી રહી છે. તેના દર્શન કરવા માટે ભાજપના પ્રમુખ આવ્યા હોવાનું જાહેરમાં કહેવામાં આવી રહ્યું છે. પણ ભાજપના અત્યંત મહત્વના રાજકીય એજન્ડા ઉપર સાધુઓ સાથે બેઠક કરવામાં આવી રહી છે. જે આવતીકાલ સુધી ચાલુ રહેશે. અમિત શાહ સાળંગપુર હનુમાનના ભક્ત રહ્યાં છે તેઓ અહીં ઘણી વખત દર્શન કરીને નીકળી જતાં હોય છે પણ આ વખતે તેઓ ૨૨ કલાક સુધી રોકાણ કરી રહ્યાં છે. અત્યંત મહત્વનું માનવામાં આવી રહ્યું છે.

૨૨ કરતાા કાફલા સાથે તેઓ અહીં આવ્યા છે. સંતમાં ભાજપના ધણા કાર્યકરો તેમનું સ્વાગત કરવા માગતા હતા પરંતુ તે તમામને સ્વાગત નહીં કરવા કહી દેવાયું છે. પરંતુ બરવાળા નગરપાલિકાના ભાજપના નેતાઓએ તલવારની ભેંટ આપીને સ્વાગત કરવાની મંજૂરી આપવામાં આવી હતી. સ્વાગત સ્વીકારી તેઓ હાઈવે પરથી જ સીધા સાળંગપુર નીકળી ગયા હતાં.

યુપીમાં ચૂંટણી જીતવી આવશ્યક

સૂત્રો કહે છે કે, ઉત્તર પ્રદેશની ચૂંટણી જીતવી ભાજપ માટે અસ્તિત્વ માટે મહત્વની છે. તેથી તે માટે જે કંઈ કરવું પડે તે કરવા તેઓ તૈયાર છે. ૨૦૦૨ પછી અહીં ભાજપની સરકાર બની નથી. જો આ ચૂંટણી જીતવામાં આવે તો રાજ્યસભામાં ભાજપની બેઠક વધે તેમ છે. અને તો જ રાજ્યસભામાં ભાજપને બહુમતી મળે તેમ છે. હાલ ઉત્તર પ્રદેશમાં ભાજપ ત્રીજા નંબર પર ચાલી રહ્યો છે. મતદારોમાં પ્રથમ પસંદગી મેળવવા માટે રામમંદિર શિવાય તેમની પાસે હવે કોઈ મુદ્દો રહેતો નથી. અહીં સરકાર બને તો જ આગામી લોકસભામાં ફરીથી સત્તા મેળવી શકાય તેમ હોવાથી યુપીને અત્યંત મહત્વની માનવામાં આવી રહી છે.

સ્વામિનારાયણ સંપ્રદાયના માઈક્રો પ્લાનિંગ પર મદાર?

ભાજપ જાણે છે કે, સ્વામિનારાયણ સંપ્રદાય ઉત્તર પ્રદેશના છપૈયા ગામ સાથે સારી રીતે જોડાયેલો છે. સ્વામિનારાયણ સંપ્રદાયના સ્વયંસેવકોનું સંગઠન અને માઈક્રો પ્લાનિંગ જ થાય છે. જ્યુમેડીસી મેદાનમાં રૂષભ ઓગસ્ટની ક્રાંતિ માટે પાટીદારોનું જે પ્લાનિંગ અને વ્યવસ્થા પણ આ સંપ્રદાયને મળતી આવતી હતી. આવું માઈક્રો પ્લાનિંગ જ પાટીદારોના યુવાન નેતાઓ કરી શકે તેમ ન હતા. ભાજપને ઉત્તર પ્રદેશમાં ચૂંટણી જીતવાની હોય તો આવા શ્રેષ્ઠ પ્લાનિંગની જરૂર છે.

હિંદુ લેબોરેટરી

હિંદુ લેબોરેટરી તરીકે પુનઃ ગુજરાતને પસંદ કરેલું છે. અગાઉ ૧૯૮૨માં બાબરી મસ્જિદ તોડીને રામમંદિર બનાવવા માટે ગુજરાતનો મહત્વનો રોલ હતો. તેમાં ગુજરાતમાં જ ટ્રેન કરાયા હતા. અડવાણીએ સોમનાથથી જ રથયાત્રા કાઢી હતી. વિશ્વએયોની ગૂંબેશ પણ ગુજરાતમાં સૌથી વધારે હતી. ગોધરાકાંડ અહીં થયો હતો. આમ ગુજરાત અહીં વતા આવ્યા છે. હવે પણ એક પ્રયોગ થાય તેવી શક્યતા છે.

યુપીની કુલ ૪૦૩ સીટ

૨૨૪	૮૦	૪૭	૨૬
એસપી	બીએસપી	બીજેપી	કોંગ્રેસ

સમાજવાદી પક્ષનાા અખિલેશ યાદવ હાલ મુખ્યમંત્રી છે. હાલ ભાજપ ત્રીજા સ્થાને બેઠકો ધરાવે છે. પ્રજા માનસમાં પણ હાલ યુપી ત્રીજા સ્થાને ભાજપ છે

◄**Image 4.6**   Headline: Did Amit Shah organize a meeting in Sarangpur to discuss the 'Ram Mandir' issue in order to win the UP elections? (Date: June 9, 2016. Paper: Sandesh. Translation of the first paragraph—in the context of the upcoming Vidhansabha elections in Uttar Pradesh in 2017, the National President of BJP, Shri Amit Shah, requested that the issue of getting a Ram temple built in Ayodhya should be the agenda for the upcoming UP elections. Immediately after announcing this, he reached Gujarat and stopped at the Hanuman temple in Sarangpur to hold meetings with the religious heads and discuss this issue. He will incorporate their opinions on what to do with the Ram temple issue and devise the party's political strategy accordingly)

regime of truth. Rutvi's parents were courteous but very uncomfortable with these discussions and asked me why these sessions were being conducted. They had signaled Rutvi not to take part in these discussions and sit there quietly. Rutvi, however, was very excited at the prospect of voicing her opinions for she had never experienced such a platform and/or class activity. She re-read the words, "should be an agenda" from the narrative, to emphasize that "… election topics are constructed around discussions related to the religious identities."

During these sessions, the courtyards held alternate voices and marginal narratives. The process of using media to restructure the character of a family space as a site where different religious bodies collided, engaged, and exchanged ideas and opinions can be identified as a very powerful form of counter-conduct. Young students were able to realize how the meaning frames they use to engage with the world are not imposed on them only by external forces; the family and the personal were all contingent to their experiences of and with the religious other. In order to change these experiences, resistance had to emerge from within the systems of governmentality that regulated their conduct in multiple ways. By defying adult expectations and participating in these discussions, Rutvi illustrated to her classmates the force of agency which lies within everybody making an individual an effective agent in the power complex. Using her voice and challenging her parents must be construed as an act of counter-conduct which changed the relational modalities prevailing in their courtyards.

In the process of generating photostories and occupying religious segregated personal spaces through newspaper reading, there was an attempt to culturally remap spaces by changing their fields of visibility and the "eccentricity of conduct" (Mill 1977). This emerged as an important form of counter-conduct among students. According to Mill, "eccentricity of conduct" is defined as a process through which an individual recognizes his/her existence as a domain of force compatible with political principle of liberty. During these cultural remapping exercises, many students challenged the system while participating in it. Each site—the street, the home, the courtyard—became a dialectical space enriched with counter-narratives and multiple voices. Students were able to discern ways, tools, techniques, and structures through which their bodies were regulated in their societies.

For instance, after we had completed these two exercises in which students were compelled to work in inter-faith groups, students from the eighth grade got occupied with the Teacher's Day celebrations. In order to create a dance group, some girls started selecting their friends not based on the dancing skills of the students but on the basis of their affection for each other. Students, therefore, approached me with two dance groups—Hindu and Muslim. When I asked them why they had created two groups, they initially didn't understand how and why their choices were such that they reinforced religious differences in the class. After probing them further, the reasons they gave for forming groups based on religious identities ranged from "we live in the same neighborhood so it will be easier to practice after school," "we can't dance with them because they are aggressive," to "my parents won't allow us to dance together." It was clear that their classroom was another important site where young students practiced their religious identities and took part in the discriminatory ideology.

We, therefore, identified classrooms as another important site to practice counter-conduct and decided to develop CML exercises which could be used to alter relational affinities and codes of conduct in the classrooms among students from both the religious communities.

Reimagining Educational Spaces Through the Creation of Body Maps

Students were assigned the project of changing the fields of visibility in the classrooms. For this to happen, classrooms had to be redesigned as contact zones—a site where disparate cultures, identities, ideologies, and experiences meet without the restraining force of the normalized structural limits imposed by authorities (Conroy 2004; Pratt 1992). Students, especially from the seventh and eighth grades, decided to change their seating arrangement and used a lottery system based on which they formed teams of three. These teams then decided to create "body maps"[3] (Davy et al. 2014) as a group project with an aim to use body maps as sites to mark their experiences [especially of discrimination] as religious subjects in the villages.

Drawing body maps helped students visualize their bodies as sites where religious power relations were inscribed and understand ways in which truth, ideologies, belief systems, mechanisms of control, and regulations were all designed keeping the body as its center. They situated their bodies at the center of their classroom spaces and picked words to demonstrate how means of conduct and practice endowed their bodies with identity markers and social expectations.

To understand this process, let us examine a "body map" designed by a group of three students.

As shown in the Image 4.7, the word *Aakramakta* [aggression] near the torso signifies ways in which young students are socialized to enact practices of aggression, both physical and verbal, against the religious other in their classrooms. Rafia explained,

> It is not us or them; I, an individual, often participate in broadening this divide between religious communities. The moment we identify our role in this situation, we realize that this pattern is common across religions, castes, and communities.

The body, as is evident, can change the constitution of a space through its conduct. Counter-conduct can be practiced by altering the mechanisms through which this body is perceived, regulated, and conducted. Counter-conduct, therefore, is not a simple disobedience of the dominant practices of conduct; it is more productive in that it suggests an alternative and tries to create conditions conducive to inaugurating this new system of governance. When students drew this body map, they produced a visual narrative to change the way they look at themselves. They focused more on the similarities between different religious bodies and created a thread explaining how each body [each student] was trained to perform its subjectivity in line with the dominant [political] rationality. Through the production of

---

[3]Body mapping is used as a tool for representing the self, using art, slogans, metaphors, and symbolism. It was first used as a visual method for eliciting responses about the self by Jane Solomon at the University of Cape Town, South Africa, as a therapy for women with HIV/AIDS and has evolved into workshops for many other diseases, traumas, and living conditions (Devine 2008; Macgregor 2009).

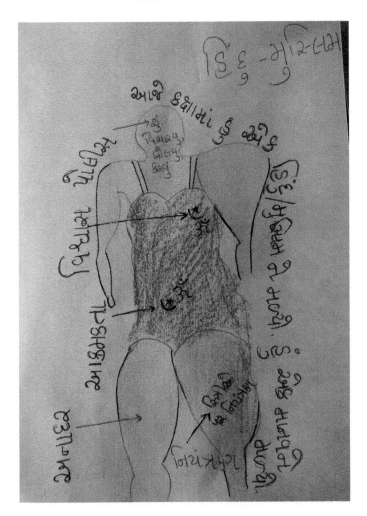

Image 4.7 Body maps created by the students

these body maps, they plot their everyday experiences onto their bodies and express it to their classmates. In one such instance, Aasita, a Hindu student from grade eight, explained,

It is difficult to express when you feel alienated because of your religion. I really like acting but most of my Hindu friends prefer to participate in dance practices. The only girl students who participate in theater are Muslims. They have different stories they share, celebrate different festivals, and have a different lifestyle. And when you are alienated by them, creating a hurdle in what you like doing, you end up hating them.

She used the word *Anadar* (disrespect) to map her experience on the body map and convey how it feels when people around you are not sensitive to your existence, i.e., the presence of your body in their environment. Designing body maps based on personal and localized experiences helped students start a conversation about how they were hurt, felt lonely, and ostracized because of their religious, caste, and gender identities. These conversations encouraged them to perform their identities and represent themselves in time and place.

As they discussed their experiences, they were encouraged to change ways in which religious bodies were located within the classroom spaces. Based on the body maps they submitted, students were asked to address the following questions:

1. Can we change the nature of this space [classrooms] by changing ways in which we use this space?
2. How can we add new meanings to this site—how and why it is used?
3. What strategies can we use to ensure that students [religious subjects] begin to experience and interact with this site and those who inhabit it differently?

While addressing these questions, students decided to change the way classroom as a site was perceived and experienced. They began with changing their seating arrangement so that there were more opportunities for students from different religious communities to interact with each other. They started sharing their meals during the recess and collaborating over study projects. Initially, they used a lot of religious motifs to decorate the walls of their classrooms. While addressing these concerns, however, they decided to treat their classrooms strictly as educational sites and decided to use "education" as a theme while planning the décor (hand drawn painting, motivational quotes, and educational articles) of the classes. A very interesting strategy they adopted was to critically analyze the kind of daily quotes they scribbled on their blackboards every morning. Initially, the quotes they selected were from religious texts and as a result students often fought while deciding which communities' religious quote will be written on the blackboard. Later, they decided to draw from the teachings of scientist, artists, poets, and revolutionary leaders such as Mahatma Gandhi and Rabindranath Tagore who emphasize on the need to create a secular country where all religions can co-exist in peace. As is evident, classroom as an educational site was effectively used to implement CML exercises with the goal of initiating some change in the affective intensities among students from different religious communities.

When students use CML exercises such as the cultural mapping techniques to examine the analytics of governmentality regulating these spaces and the religious bodies, they begin to understand how the conduct of space is enacted through specific forms of interaction of bodies within those boundaries. When these interactions change in terms of who can occupy those spaces, who can wield control, and what/who is visible through and in these spaces, the discourse changes and power relations are challenged.

In the next section, we elaborate on how these regimes of knowledge are contingent with the dominant political rationality, reinforced by those who have access to and claim power over modes and techniques of conduct.

ANALYZING REGIMES OF TRUTH–KNOWLEDGE

Regimes of knowledge refers to the ways in which a space, an individual, a phenomenon, or a belief is converted into an object of inquiry and, in the process, made a part of a dominant system of political rationality. Developing media education exercises in which students from only one community have an authorial role over representations for a fixed period of time can be an effective way for students to realize how regimes of truth and knowledge are reified and reinforced through practices and conduct of individuals. Critical media literacy provides the required resources to create this experience of induced discrimination without actually jeopardizing the well-being of the students by placing them in real-life situations of inequality. It affords the creation of a mediated environment where students can temporarily map themselves within the prevailing conditions of the society and understand how their bodies, emotions, experiences, and interactions can be influenced by political, religious, and cultural forces.

In order to create an experience of being discriminated against, and to compel them to operate from the margins while resisting the dominant rationality, we designed CML exercises to display the consequences of the acts of micro-aggression on individual minds and bodies. This exercise was titled *Kona Shabdo, kone maate* (whose words and for whom). The pedagogical principle underpinning this exercise involved "upsetting the rules of representation" (O'Brien and Szeman 2004). This exercise involves two steps: first, compelling students to enter states of experience where they can define the role, character, and circumstances of an individual in the process of creating representations; second, providing them with the necessary skills to produce counter-narratives and challenge naturalized modes and forms of representation for greater inclusivity of different voices in their lived realities.

For this, students in a classroom were divided into two groups based on their religious identities. As a result, we had two groups in each class—a Hindu team and a Muslim team. Each group was assigned the authorial role to represent the other group under two different circumstances, i.e., when they had no interactions with the other group compared to when they were asked to interact with them before producing these narratives. Each group in the authorial role was given the following themes based on which they were supposed to create media narratives—newspaper articles, videos, photostories, and so on based on local stories in their village (Table 4.2).

When students were allowed to work together based on their religious affiliations, it created a lot of confusion among them; we had always discouraged them from identifying themselves as religious monoliths and to look for interests, qualities, and identities in the religious other that could help them bond with their classmates. In this case, however, we wanted to help them understand how having an authorial role, i.e., a position of power, devoid of critical skills to acknowledge differences, translates into reification of the dominant rationality through production of conventional narratives. Let us look at a narrative created by a group of Hindu students

Table 4.2 Themes for content creation

S. no.	Themes
1.	Festival/s celebrated by the community
2.	Economic and education characteristics of the community
3.	Political preferences of the community
4.	Influence of religion on the lives of the community members

about their Muslim classmates on the theme—influence of religion on the lives of community members.

This narrative was created without interacting with the community members who were being represented. As is evident, the narrative is biased and based on an incomplete understanding of the religious other. When this narrative was presented in the class and displayed on the class board, it created a lot of unrest among the Muslim students. They were angry at how their religion and religious practices were labeled as "aggressive" and "violent." Also, they were not allowed to contest these representations and provide alternate accounts for a considerable amount of time. The Muslim students, however, couldn't stop themselves from discussing the innate biases in this narrative. Zakir, a Muslim student, was heard talking to his friend during the recess where he said,

> These representations are partial. They don't represent us. They represent what the Hindus think of us. Also, they have never attended these classes. We are also taught about *aman* (peace), love, and respect.

When Muslim students experienced the state of being voiceless, they were uncomfortable with the situation and wanted to change the team producing these narratives. Many students approached me requesting that groups be formed in such a way that students from their community had equal representation in the content that was being curated for the classroom board. When they were refused to do so, Muslim students in other groups created an equally biased and uncritical narrative about the Hindu community on the theme "Political preferences of the community."

What is evident from this analysis is how young students who are raised in an exclusionary environment wherein multiple voices cannot engage in deliberative dialogues, negotiate differences, and address common concerns find it difficult to enact civic engagement as their social responsibility toward upholding principles of equality. In a society where the minority voices are marginalized or silenced by the force of the majoritarianism of any kind, civic engagement becomes a way of asserting their social identities—religious, caste, class, gender, and others. In this situation of induced discrimination, for instance, students felt the need to assert their voices by creating biased representations of the other in order to reinforce the position of their community in the classrooms. It is, therefore, crucial to acknowledge that when students are encouraged to create narratives and representations based on lived experiences without initiating dialogues between various stakeholders concerning a particular narrative, the results can sometimes be problematic (Fleetwood 2005).

In order to create inclusive narratives, students must be placed in situations and experiences that allow them to understand how they are constituted as [religious] subjects. According to Lorenzini (2016), regimes of knowledge implicate subjects to accept the authority of a single truth and thus vow their submission to it. This process of "self-constitution" requires the subjects to conduct themselves according to a certain true discourse that is upheld in their societies in order to demonstrate how they construct themselves as subjects of the regime of knowledge they verbalize. In other words, the regime of truth and knowledge in which the Hindu/Muslim adolescents are constituted as subjects allows them to access people and experiences that are beyond the boundaries of physical intimacy through a given perceptive representational frame.

In the village, for instance, the existence, opinions, voice, and experiences of the Hindu "other" may remain inaccessible to a Muslim child in a number of ways—they seldom engage in conversations with one another, they refuse to participate in and discuss each other's concerns, they are unable to forge productive ties to explore the contours of each other's lived experiences, and so on. They rely extensively on the representations available to them in the possible fields of thoughts and actions to access the religious other and reinforce these through their actions in their interactions with the "other." The process of de-neutralizing the systems of meaning-making and representation begins with providing students with learning opportunities and critical thinking tools which would help them identify their regimes of truth and knowledge as essentially historical, contingent rather than absolute and all encompassing.

When students are asked to critically examine how they submit themselves to systems of governmentality by operating in accordance with the naturalized truth discourses, they learn to identify power relations inherent to this process. This enables them to engage in new alterities by making explicit how changing the politics by which we think and act can change the conduct. In the second phase of the CML exercise *Kona shabado, koni maate*, for instance, we created groups consisting of students from both the religious communities to ensure that the authorial role was shared which brought into force two competing regimes of truth and knowledge. When Hindu and Muslim students were selected as teammates, they entered a creative moment in their subjectification process. In this, students were inclined to look for new ways of representing the religious other and alternate modes of enacting their subjectivity. For instance, in one such group a participant was heard engaging with her teammates as she emphasized,

> Any representation, either in the form of a video, photo or news narratives that our group produces must take into account the sentiments and opinions of all the group members. Both the Hindu and Muslim groups have experienced feelings of neglect when the other group built on their own opinions without taking into consideration the other's lived experiences. Now that we have members from both the religious communities we should learn to incorporate diverse voices and create a narrative.

One such inter-religious group created a video on the theme "Influence of religion on the lives of the community members." Interestingly, they were keen on appropriating a popular regional song *Sonu tane maara par bharoso nai kae*[4] (Sonu, am I not trustworthy?) and rewriting the lyrics to satirize instances of religious discrimination in their village (Table 4.3).

The students worked as bricoleurs who use signs and images from the popular media culture to resist and redefine the dominant trends prevailing in the society. According to Poyntz (2006), the critical potential of such student videos lies in the tensions between the value of the production work as a means of self-expression and its implications in the socio-cultural environments the adolescents inhabit. This is because the process of defining and representing a community exposes students to the power structures prevalent in their societies and how the contingent socio-cultural practices organize and limit those communities. For instance, in recontextualizing a popular local song to verbalize and represent their lived experiences of religious discrimination, students were constructing and performing an alternate self-identity (Willet 2008).

As was the case, while composing this song both Hindu and Muslim students identified the discriminatory practices they had experienced in their village and this initiated a discussion on caste differences as well. In one of the verses of the song (refer to Table 4.2), students describe how they are raised by their communities in ways which create in them a sense of aversion for the lifestyle choices of members of a different religion leading to acts

---

[4]The original *Sonu* song was composed by Ajay Kshirsagar in Marathi and in days went viral and has inspired many satirical spinoffs.
(https://www.huffingtonpost.in/2017/07/26/meet-ajay-kshirsagar-the-creator-of-the-insanely-viral-sonu-tu_a_23048830/).

Table 4.3 Translation for the song "Sonu"

Sonu—Am I not trustworthy?
Sonu, why don't you trust me?
Is it because my eating habits are different,
I like having chicken curry with *rotis*,
These rotis are so full and round,
Sonu, why don't you talk to me lovingly?

Sonu, why don't you trust me?
You abuse me so much,
You slap my face frequently,
But have you seen how innocent my round face is?
Sonu, why don't you talk to me lovingly?

Sonu, why don't you trust me?
Though I speak a different language,
But I have always nice things to say,
Have you seen how round the shape of my mouth is?
Sonu, why don't you talk to me lovingly?

Sonu, why don't you trust me?
We all are the citizens of one country,
Our flag has the Ashoka chakra in it,
Have you seen how round the chakra is?
Sonu, why don't you talk to me lovingly?

of micro-aggression in classrooms. Discussing this issue in a light-hearted satirical manner through video production helped students to identify their role in perpetuating religious discrimination as they experienced the other from within the boundaries of their regimes of truth and knowledge.

Such activities entail two analytical moments—first, they situate students within the narrative practices of storytelling and develop their technical competencies, and second, they help students analyze how these narratives emerge from and reinforce the power–knowledge complex.

Many scholars such as Giroux (1992, 1994), McLaren (1995), and Lankshear (1997) have drawn inspiration from the critical thought of Freire and Foucault and identified classrooms as sites for the construction of alternate regimes of knowledge and transformative cultural, moral, and political identities. They emphasize that within classrooms, educators can help students challenge the ritual inscriptions of the imposed religious/political identities and design interventions to create a fraying around the edges of the naturalized relations of power. For this to happen, classrooms must act as contact zones—a site where disparate cultures, identities, ideologies, and experiences meet without the restraining force of the normalized structural limits imposed by authorities (Conroy 2004; Pratt 1992). In other words, a classroom should exist as a liminal space which lies beyond the taken-for-granted normality of everyday experiences wherein there is a reformulation of the learner's meaning frame (Schwartzman 2010) and a friction is created in the learner's subjectivity (Land et al. 2014). Many studies have successfully deployed inventive ways to reimagine classrooms and education as fluid sites which allow students to question their subjectivity and replenish it with new perspectives and learnings. For instance, Meyer and Land (2005) used the theory of liminality to create conceptual getaways in classroom teaching which helped their students perform a progressive function by encountering and integrating something new to their already existing understanding. This involves "… envisaging of an alternate version of the self which is contemplated through the threshold space" (Land et al. 2014). According to them, creating alternate regimes of knowledge requires infusing classrooms with intended moments of creativity and fluidity which disclose alternative positions of thinking, understanding, and being, and equip young students with critical reflective dispositions to adopt and occupy these positions of otherness. When students were involved in creative activities in which working, interacting, and accepting the "other" was a *sine qua non* condition, they were able to conceptualize an ontological space and an epistemological position where the codes of religious status and power structures do not apply.

Students were able to acquire a *liminal personae* as members of a temporary community of classmates (Donnan and Wilson 1999). This new identity is articulated through team norms created by the members, often based on the dissolution and undoing of normative categories. When Hindu and Muslim students worked together, they agreed to borrow from diverse knowledge structures and present a more comprehensive analysis. They were more attentive to the experiences of the other—listening to stories from within a different community was not only fascinating for them but also helped them feel a lot closer to the realities of the religious other. Muslim students rectified some false representations of their community in these narratives as they introduced the Hindu students to their lifestyle choices. According to a Muslim student Najma, for instance, many Muslims were ill-informed about many Hindu festivals as they considered it abominable to engage in discussions related to the followers of a lesser god. She explains,

It is extremely difficult to be an insider and deal with people who are rigid and refuse to even explore different possibilities. I come from a liberal family background; my best friend is a Hindu and we spend a lot of time together. I, therefore, know more about Hindu festivals than my other Muslim class-mates. Had it not been for a group project where students were encouraged to produce media narratives together, students would have never felt a need to know the other, to understand where they come from. Just yesterday, as we sat discussing Diwali, a Hindu girl said, "Well, all festivals mark a triumph of good over evil; only the protagonist changes. In one version of Ramayan,[5] Rama is hailed as God and in yet another Ravan is the hero. Whose truth should be upheld?" This made us think and we realized that truth can be used to create a community and hold it together.

While engaging with each other, learning to disagree with one another respectfully, and giving space for multiple experiences to be voiced, students learnt to be critically empathetic toward the religious other.

When students created this narrative, they borrowed from the conventions of writing a newspaper article as they localized the text and rendered it accessible to other classmates such that it could become a part of their alternate regime of knowledge. In learning how to appropriate media technologies to narrate stories about issues that influence their communities (Jankowski 2002), they introduced an analysis of a new level of abstraction, i.e., the concept of truth, when they asked questions such as: How can people and ideas be represented? Whose regimes of knowledge are reified through such representations? and How these representations influence the way we engage with the "other"? Before producing a media text, these groups critically analyzed how a representation defines/limits the role of both the enunciator and the enunciated and how it formulates the relation between subjects and their communities in which they are socialized. While producing the Sonu video, for instance, students created a worksheet that is illustrated in Table 4.4.

Questions raised in this worksheet were inspired by the preliminary CML exercises students participated in where they were introduced to the concepts of critical reading and the politics of freedom (Freire 1973; Masterman 1985). They were taught to problematize the text and de-neutralize its content by asking questions such as: Who created the text, for whom, for what purposes, and how will it be received? They used this exercise

---

[5] Ramayana is a popular epic/religious text in South and Southeast Asia.

Table 4.4   Core critical media education Questions

Who will create this text? Hindus and Muslims working together as teammates **How do we truthfully represent voices from both these communities?** We must draw from the experiences of all the teammates. Each member will write how they faced discrimination due to their religious identities and then we will sift through the content gathered to choose examples which best represent the communities **How can we make our participation more inclusive?** We must allow each member to work as an author as well as a character in the text. In this way, we will be in a better position to understand how to voice the concerns of those being represented in a text **Who is our target audience and what is our goal?** We want to ensure that our classmates get access to local narratives that highlight voices of both communities in conversation with one another

to analyze the process of media production and how it was embedded in local politics, multiple discourses, sedimented social identities, and cultural practices propagated by the dominant rationality. Through critical reading practices, students were able to create fluid boundaries in their roles as an author and a subject of the text. They decided to assume both the roles alternatively because they felt the need to bridge the gap between the enunciator and the enunciated. Priyal, a Hindu student from grade eight, explained,

> It is sometimes important to realize the immense power that authors possess through the characters they create. Also, these representations have some real life consequences for individuals, in that, they are not fictional. We are talking about newspaper articles that influence the formation of a public opinion. When this very same author enters the role of a subject who has no power whatsoever in how and why he is represented, it is possible that the author might feel more responsible and may evaluate the outcomes of the representations they create and circulate.

As is demonstrated through this exercise, though the ability to speak the truth, to represent it, and to own it lies in the hands of those who are sanctioned to exercise power by the mechanisms, techniques, and discourses of governmentality, it can be challenged. Based on what the students experienced, it is apparent that the "general politics of truth" can be problematized if students share the power over the content being produced and the representations between circulated. When Hindu–Muslim students collectively created content on political issues they realized that it was not an innocent activity. Shraddha, an eighth grade student, said,

> When we were writing a newspaper report on political issues concerning both Hindus and Muslims in our village we realized that it is a sensitive topic and any major lapse on our part might deeply hurt others and escalate into a fight. Also, each community tried very hard to ensure that they had a stronger voice in the narratives created. Working together in no way meant we had forgotten all about our differences; that isn't possible. What was important, however, is this need we experienced to listen to others and to try as much as possible to ensure that one community didn't feel as if they had no stake in the process.

In order to illustrate how this process unfolded, let us take the example of a media text created by a group of Muslim students, emphasizing that girls from the Hindu community are less educated and often married off early. This was partly because according to them, the Hindus in their village were very regressive and didn't believe in treating their girl children with respect whereas their own religion upheld women rights. Many Hindu students had reservations about such representations and questioned the media producers. Given under is a conversation between Hindu and Muslim students during one such discussion regarding the representation of the role of girls in the Hindu community.

> *Poonam (Hindu student)*: Women in our community are not always oppressed. We are not allowed to visit temples only during some days of the month for hygiene purposes. The role of women in our community is more than just what you have presented through this media text.
>
> *Sohail (Muslim student)*: We feel Hindu women and girls are less inclined to study and join high school. Most of our Muslim girls are allowed to pursue higher education; Nausheen won the best student award this year.
>
> *Ramesh (Hindu student)*: Isn't this the case with girls from your community as well? Many Muslim girls are not allowed to attend school and even if they are not officially married at a young age their parents do get them engaged while they are still in grade eight. Don't you remember how Salma stopped coming to school and within days we realized that she was married?
>
> *Poonam (Hindu student)*: This is a common problem with both the communities—girls are not allowed to pursue higher education. There is no use blaming one community.

Though the Muslim students were reluctant, they had to rewrite the narrative and take into consideration the views, aspirations, and expectations of their classmates and team members. Given below are the two narratives drafted by the students. The first, illustrated in Table 4.5, was created by a group of Muslim students based exclusively on their own perspectives and opinions and in the other, i.e., Table 4.6, some Hindu students worked with their Muslim classmates to create an inclusive newspaper article.

This was possible because the hierarchical relationship between the enunciator and the enunciated was problematized, and the author(s) and their politics of truth were rendered accessible to the audience. Rishika, a Hindu student from class seven, discussed this exercise and suggested that

Table 4.5   Media narrative created by Muslim students

Dropout rate higher among Hindu girls in the village
Date: September 9, 2017
The current trends in the village indicate that Hindu girls are more likely to dropout of school after completing their primary education. Many Hindu girls from the village are not allowed to pursue higher education and are married early
This has taken a toll on their community and created a regressive attitude among the Hindus. They are more concerned about their religion than ever before and prioritize their belief system over ideas of growth and progress

Table 4.6   A narrative created by Hindu students

Girls are not allowed to pursue higher education in the village
Date: September 28, 2017
Many girls in the village are likely to dropout of schools after completing their primary education. There are many constraints which the girls experience in their struggle to enroll for higher education in schools and colleges
This is because many villager elders contend that if girls are "over-educated" they might not be able to assimilate in new families when they get married. "Also, highly educated girls have a loose character and are more prone to fall prey to temptations," says Fazal Sheikh, the maulvi of the village mosque. Similarly, many other village residents feel that girls should be trained to look after their families and stay at home. According to Namitaben, a 45 year old woman in the village, "Girls are considered to be home-makers. Educated them and then they are ready to break the house"
There are some liberal voices in the village community as well who are striving to promote the "*Beti Bachao, Beti Padhao*" movement. One of the members of the Panchayat says that it is very important for girls to be educated if they are to live an independent and a dignified life. Many social problems such as domestic violence, alcohol abuse, and the consumption of tobacco can be tackled if women of the houses are educated and smart

the boundaries between who gets to produce media narratives and who receives these narratives must be open and fluid. She explained,

> When authors realize that they are equally vulnerable to being represented in a bad light by others, they are more sensitive and act responsibly. This exercise puts authors in a situation of discomfort and forces them to think and create from beyond what they have seen and experienced.

A crucial point in both Shraddha's and Rishika's accounts of their experience is the claim that media literacy exercises are not always liberating, in that, they don't actually alter the interiority of individuals and influence the way they think, act, and behave outside these induced experiences of collaborative learning in the classrooms. It brings our attention back to how overly celebratory claims about the role of critical media literacy can be misleading. During these classroom activities, some students intentionally expressed and conducted themselves in accordance with social expectations created through our presence as media educators in the classroom. An association of three long years had allowed them to access our thoughts, actions and ideologies. According to media education scholars such as Braggs (2007), Fleetwood (2005), and Orner (1992), an unending expectation from the young people to engage in processes of self-expression in public forums where the presence of others acts as a regulating force can lead to the emergence of a culture where youth conduct is regulated and monitored. We had to, therefore, be constantly reflexive of our role as media educators and create moments of doubts in their minds where they were confused about our value systems. While interacting with them and asking them questions related to religious discrimination in the village, we had to sometimes assure them in a sympathetic tone that their thoughts and behavior, however radical or discriminatory, will be respected and listened to. We were able to access their regimes of knowledge only when we acknowledged the burden of these inevitable differences between the students and the educators and learnt to be sensitive toward their culture and practices. We had to stand guard against the possibility that the meta-narrative of religious harmony might start functioning hegemonically and jeopardize the principal tenets of critical education on which this project was conceived.

In order to create such an open space in the classrooms and guide students toward identifying the counter-hegemonic forms of media agency, we have borrowed from the works of Luke (2002), Kellner (1998, 2002), and Lewis and Jhally (1998), who suggest that media literacy must be envisioned as a democratic process and a project of social justice that enables students to enact their role as responsible citizens. Though many scholars such as Buckingham (2003), Hobbs (1998, 2008), Hobbs and Jensen (2009) suggest that the most important role of a media educator is to prepare their students to operate in media saturated environments and not create critical, sophisticated "citizens" out of them, we believe otherwise. Creating a friction in the regimes of knowledge is not an apolitical process and requires students to acknowledge their stake as active and critical citizens/residents of their communities. Our experiences with students in these villages have made us realize the need to subject young students to critical analysis as a way of enhancing a sense of reflexivity and agency in them. It is important to embrace strategies of critical analysis which include examining forms of self-expression by students and repositions a media educator as someone who doesn't merely "make" creative and competitive individuals but also channelizes young students' engagement with the power structures (Goldfarb 2002; Luke 2002) This can enable students to visualize media representations that reside in alternate, counter-hegemonic regimes of knowledge.

Many students who participated in the CML exercise designed to challenge the existing/dominant regimes of knowledge stressed on the importance of talking to each other as a way of fostering a sense of empathy and a culture of care. When they talk to each other, they enter a space in which they are able to identify their differences and can try to bridge them. According to various scholars such as Arendt (1978), Bakhtin (1981), Freire (1976), and Dewey (1954), in order to recognize one's position in the world, form identities, and relate with others, it is important to form opinions about oneself in relation to others. This process of forming opinion, however, must be a dynamic process that is replenished, redefined, and reconstructed with new experiences and critical inquiry. This is possible only when individuals encounter others and engage with the differences they present. This process requires that we learn to judge, we learn to involve ourselves in "a talking through, bringing forth, a constant engagement with one's own thoughts and that of others" (Silverstone 2007). If students are to create alternate representations they have to learn to be critical and reflective of and reciprocal to others in their societies. Accordingly the third dimension of the counter-conduct framework emphasizes on the need to devise a technology of counter-conduct in learning for creating alternate ontological space and epistemological practices which privilege the discursive and spatial concepts of critical distancing from the text (Poyntz 2015), co-occupying classrooms, entering alternate forms of subjectivities, and engendering interaction through teamwork and collaborative learning activities among bodies limited by religious identities. In this book, we argue that dialogic practices of engagement can be deployed as a technology of counter-conduct because they are rooted in democratic strategies of participation and preserve the autonomy of all the stakeholders participating in the process. In the next chapter, we explain how this form of engagement practices can help students experiment with new forms of association and redefine their identities to include facets of experience that lie beyond their immediate socio-cultural and mediated realities. Following the same theoretical trajectory, we demonstrate in the next chapter that the fourth dimension of the counter-conduct framework, i.e., a change in subjective identities, is coterminous with young students learning to operate in a dialogical space wherein alternate modes of experiencing the world [in conversation with others] are activated.

REFERENCES

Amin, A. (2010). *Land of strangers.* Cambridge: Polity Press.

Arendt, H. (1958). *The human condition.* London: The University of Chicago Press.

Arendt, H. (1978). *The life of mind.* New York: Harcourt Brace Jovanovich.

Bakhtin, M. (1981). Discourse in the novel. In M. Holquist (Ed.), *The dialogic imagination: Four essays by M. M. Bakhtin* (pp. 259–422). Austin: University of Texas Press.

Bennett, W. L. (2008). Changing citizenship in the digital age. In W. L. Bennett (Ed.), *Civic life online: Learning how digital media can engage youth* (pp. 1–24). Cambridge: MIT Press.

Braggs, S. (2007). 'Student voice' and governmentality: The production of enterprising subjects? *Discourse: Studies in the Cultural Politics of Education, 28*(3), 343–358.

Buckingham, D. (2003). *Media education: Literacy, learning and contemporary culture.* Cambridge: Polity Press.

Buckingham, D., Niesyto, H., & Fisherkeller, J. (2003). Videoculture: Crossing borders with young people's video productions. *Television and New Media, 4*(4), 461–482.

Buckingham, D., & Sefton-Green, J. (2003). Gotta catch'em all: Structure, agency and pedagogy in children's media culture. *Media, Culture and Society, 25*(3), 379–399.

Conroy, J. (2004). *Betwixt and between: The liminal imagination, education and democracy.* New York: Peter Lang.

Davidson, A. (2011). In praise of counter-conduct. *History of Human Sciences, 24*(4), 25–41.

Davy, C., Magalhaes, L., Mandich, A., & Galheigo, S. (2014). Aspects of the resilience and settlement of refugee youth: A narrative study using body maps. *UFSCar, 22*(2), 231–241.

Dean, M. (1999). *Governmentality: Power and rule in modern society.* London: Sage.

Devine, C. (2008). The moon, the stars, and a scar: Body mapping stories of women living with HIV/AIDS. *Border Crossings, 27*(2), 58–65.

Dewey, J. (1954). *The public and its problems.* Athens, OH: Swallow Press.

Donnan, H., & Wilson, T. (1999). *Borders: Frontiers of identity, nation and state.* London: Bloomsbury.

Fleetwood, N. (2005). Authenticating practices: Producing realness, performing youth. In S. Maira & E. Seop (Eds.), *Youthscapes: The popular, the national, the global* (pp. 155–172). Philadelphia: University of Pennsylvania Press.

Foucault, M. (1982). The subject and power. *Critical Inquiry, 8*(4), 777–795.

Foucault, M. (1997). *Discipline and punish: The birth of the prison* (A. Sheridan, Trans.). New York: Random House.

Foucault, M. (2007). *Security, territory, population: Lectures at the Collège de France 1977–1978.* Basingstoke: Palgrave Macmillan.

Freire, P. (1970). *Pedagogy of the oppressed.* New Delhi: Penguin Books.

Freire, P. (1973). *Education for critical consciousness.* New York, NY: Seabury Press.

Freire, P. (1976). *Education, the practice of freedom.* New York: Writers and Readers Publishing Cooperative.

Giddens, A. (1984). *The constitution of society.* Cambridge, UK: Polity Press.

Giroux, H. (2001). *Public spaces, private lives: Beyond the culture of cynicism.* Lanham, MD: Rowman & Littlefield.

Giroux, H. A. (1992). *Border crossings: Cultural workers and the politics of education.* New York: Routledge.

Giroux, H. A. (1994). *Disturbing pleasures: Learning popular culture.* New York: Routledge.

Goldfarb, B. (2002). *Visual pedagogy: Media cultures in and beyond the classroom.* Durham: Duke University Press.

Held, D. (2002). The transformation of political community: Rethinking democracy in the context of globalization. In N. Dower & J. Williams (Eds.), *Global citizenship: A critical introduction* (pp. 92–100). New York: Routledge.

Heller, K. (1996). Power, subjectification and resistance in Foucault. *SubStance, 25*(1), 78–110.

Hobbs, R. (1998). The seven great debates in the media literacy movement. *Journal of Communication, 48*(1), 16–32.

Hobbs, R., & Jensen, A. (2009). The past, present and future of media literacy education. *The Journal of Media Literacy Education, 1*, 1–11.

Hoechsmann, M., & Poyntz, S. (2012). *Media literacies: A critical introduction.* Chichester: Wiley-Blackwell.

Hutchings, K. (2002). Feminism and global citizenship. In N. Dower & J. Williams (Eds.), *Global citizenship: A critical introduction* (pp. 30–40). New York: Routledge.

Jankowski, N. (2002). Creating community with media: History, theories and scientific investigations. In L. S. Lievrouw & S. M. Livingstone (Eds.), *Handbook of new media: Social shaping and consequences of ICTs* (pp. 34–49). Thousand Oaks: Sage.

Kellner, D. (1998). Multiple literacies and critical pedagogy in a multicultural society. *Educational Theory, 48*(1), 103–123.

Kirmani, N. (2008). Competing constructions of "Muslim-ness" in the South Delhi neighborhood of Zakir Nagar. *Journal of Muslim Minority Affairs, 28*(3), 355–370.

Land, R., Rattray, J., & Vivian, P. (2014). Learning in the liminal space: A semiotic approach to threshold concepts. *High Educ, 67*, 199–217.

Lankshear, C. (1997). *Changing literacies, changing education.* New York: Open University Press.

Lewis, J., & Jhally, S. (1998). The struggle over media literacy. *Journal of Communication, 48*(1), 1–8.

Lorenzini, D. (2016). From counter-conduct to critical attitude: Michel Foucault and the art of not being governed quite so much. *Foucault Studies, 21*, 7–21.

Luke, C. (2002). Cyber-schooling and technological change: Multiple literacies for new times. In B. Cope & M. Kalantzis (Eds.), *Multiliteracies: Literacy learning and the design of social futures* (pp. 69–91). London: Routledge.

Macgregor, N. H. (2009). Mapping the body: Tracing the personal and the political dimensions of HIV/AIDs in Khayelitsha, South Africa. *Anthropology & Medicine, 16*(1), 85–95.

Malmvig, H. (2016). Eyes wide shut: Power and creative counter-conducts in the battle for Syria, 2011–2014. *Global Society.* https://doi.org/10.1080/13600826.2016.1150810.

Masterman, L. (1985). *Teaching the media.* London: Comedia Publishing Group.

McLaren, P. (1995). *Critical pedagogy and predatory culture: Oppositional politics in a postmodern era.* New York, NY: Routledge.

Meyer, J., & Land, R. (2005). *Overcoming barriers to student understanding: Threshold concepts and troublesome knowledge.* London and New York: Routledge.

Mill, J. S. M. (1977). On liberty. In J. M. Robson (Ed.), *The collected works of John Stuart Mill* (Vol. XVIII). Toronto and London: University of Toronto Press.

O'Brien, S., & Szeman, I. (2004). *Popular culture: A user's guide.* Scarborough: Nelson.

Orner, M. (1992). Interrupting the calls for student voice in libratory education: A feminist poststructuralist perspective. In C. Luke & J. Gore (Eds.), *Feminisms and critical pedagogy* (pp. 15–25). New York: Routledge.

Pathak-Shelat, M. (2014). *Global civic engagement on online platforms: Women as transcultural citizens* (Unpublished dissertation). University of Wisconsin-Madison, Madison.

Poyntz, S. (2006). Independent media, youth agency, and the promise of media education. *Canadian Journal of Education, 29*(1), 154–175.

Poyntz, S. (2015). Conceptual futures: Thinking and the role of key concept models in media literacy education. *Media Education Research Journal, 6*(1), 63–79.

Pratt, M. (1992). Arts of the contact zone. *Modern Language Association, 5*(8), 33–40.

Rose, N. (1999). *Powers of freedom: Reframing political thought.* Cambridge: Cambridge University Press.

Schwartzman, L. (2010). Transcending disciplinary boundaries: A proposed theoretical foundation for threshold concepts. In J. H. F. Meyer, R. Land, & C. Baillie (Eds.), *Threshold concepts and transformational learning* (pp. 21–44). Rotterdam: Sense Publishing.

Sefton-Green, J. (2006). Youth, technology and media cultures. *Review of Research in Education, 30,* 279–306.

Silverstone, R. (2007). *Media and morality: On the rise of the Mediapolis.* Cambridge: Polity Press.

Soep, E. (2006). Beyond literacy and voice in youth media education. *McGill Journal of Education, 41*(3), 197–213.

Sokhi-Bulley, B. (2016). Re-reading the riots: Counter-conduct in London 2011. *Global Society.* https://doi.org/10.1080/13600826.2016.1143348.

Willet, R. (2008). Consumer citizens online: Structure, agency, and gender in online participation. In D. Buckingham (Ed.), *Youth, identity and digital media* (pp. 49–69). Cambridge: MIT Press.

CHAPTER 5

Media Education as Counter-Conduct: Developing Dialogic Practices and Analyzing Change in Subjectivities

Abstract In this chapter, dialogic practices of engagement are identified as a technology of counter-conduct because they are rooted in democratic strategies of participation and preserve the autonomy of all the stakeholders participating in the process. These practices are deployed to enable students to acknowledge why and how their subjective identities influence their classroom participation and their attitude toward the "religious other." As a result, students experience alternate subjectivities and often require a platform to enact/act out their newly acquired identities. In this chapter, we demonstrate how theater can be appropriated for creating a new reality and a new set of experiences in and through a story to subvert particular forms of action. We demonstrate how as children enact the role of the "other," the dominant rationality is disturbed, their subjectification is challenged, and they are encouraged to study the coalition of multiple contexts in which the performance was conceived and enacted.

Keywords Technology of counter-conduct · Dialogic practices · Deconstructive reading · Semantic networks · Theater · Alternate identities

INTRODUCTION

In the previous chapters, we discussed how students are constituted as subjects of religious politics, how they are predisposed to the governmentality of power/knowledge structures and regimes of practices, and how their conduct is regulated by juridical strategies. The resultant analysis revealed the mutually constitutive relationship between governance and resistance, power and freedom, and conduct and counter-conduct. Drawing on the framework of counter-conduct, we delineated resistance practices deployed by students to reimagine the fields of visibility in their villages and challenge the regimes of truth/knowledge they inhabit. These counter-practices, however, require an effective technè of self, a technology of counter-conduct in learning, to sustain an ontological space of microdisruption wherein alternative epistemological practices may emerge. The third dimension of the counter-conduct framework discusses the need of cultivating a technè of self that helps students critically engage with naturalized rituals, i.e., norms and practices of conduct that create of them a conformist subject, subscribing to a posteriori perception that truth is a generalizable universal. Dialogic practices of engagement, therefore, have been identified in this book as a technology of counter-conduct because they are rooted in democratic strategies of participation and preserve the autonomy of all the stakeholders participating in the process.

DIALOGIC PRACTICES AS THE TECHNÈ OF SELF

Students operate in and occupy spaces that are constituted by a dissonance of voices defined as the diverse modalities of their religious identities and experiences. When religious identities become the channel through which the world is experienced, students "exoticize" the religious other based on an abject differentiation, pushing other voices on the borderlines of the dominant culture, i.e., the truth regimes they inhabit. As illustrated in earlier chapters, this appropriation of the religious other based on axiomatics for sustaining a dominant rationality of religious discrimination translates into a disapprobation of an ethic of heterogeneity which is nestled in an appreciation of differences. Let us take as an example the classroom interactions between Hindu and Muslim students. When we started conducting media education classes in the *primary school*, students from the Muslim community showed a complete disregard for their Hindu classmates while practicing for theater projects and vice versa. Students often disregarded the request put forth by their classmates from the other religious communities with regard to practice schedules, content creation, role assignments, and so on. They clearly did not see a need for consulting or discussing with their teammates from a different religious community and in doing so uphold the institutionalized logic of a perceived unity in identity. They were empathetic only toward the suggestions and requests put forth by their community members.

What is evident from this discussion is that their religious identity is their universal truth, i.e., religious identities encompass their lived realities and provide them with a means to access the material world. Mahima, a Hindu student from grade seven, explained, "Being a Hindu means you get to experience everything as a Hindu. My life outcomes, my social relations, my schooling and marriage, everything is prefixed on my religious identity. It is important for me to see the world as a Hindu because this is something that has been bestowed upon me by my God." When probed about other social identities that might be of significance to her experiences as a citizen of the country, she added, "Yes, other identities matter but they stem from my belief system, from my religious identity. My social status as a Thakur girl, the activities I engage in such as reading, watching TV, listening to radio, and so on strengthen my social bonding with others in my religious community. It is difficult for me to think beyond my religion and go against the society." Like Mahima, most of the other students from the school articulated their experiences as facets of their religious identities and reinforced a manichean symmetrization of subjective identities as positive and negative. For Muslim students, their Hindu classmates were the followers of *saitan* and for the Hindu students their Muslim classmates were aggressive, violent, and belonged to a community which created terrorists.

As we continued interacting with students in the role of their media educators, we felt a need to open up a plethora of subject positions inherent in their religious identities and use a de-archiving method (Foucault 1973) to help them appreciate the contextual dependency of their interpretations of the religious other. We wanted to identify ways to create fissures in their rigid "moral" standards for judging and representing the other through the everyday discourses circulated in their communities.

Dialogic practices, in this project, are thus defined as critical engagement strategies which enable students to reanalyze their religious identities as an ontological space produced by and containing references to variegated socio-cultural and political experiences. According to Per Linell (1998,

2003), such dialogic practices of engagement are not so much regarding "others" as they are about how we come to know and interact with "others." Dialogic practices involve an inward approach where students learn that the truth about the religious other is never a fixed meaning. Engagement with "others" is never a static process producing fixed meanings; it is a dialogue that can be reconfigured if we change human practices related to the space and time, or use a different interpretive framework in the meaning-making process (Bakhtin 1986).

Taking the example of chronotope, Bakhtin explores this "alternate space" marked by dialogism as reinforcing a lack of finality in the articulation of identity in discourses. According to this theoretical exegesis, students should be encouraged to

1. Create new social identities in and through the dialogue they engage in with the religious other (Identify in dialogue);
2. Analyze how reimagining conditions of possibility can create fissures in their subjective identities (Intersubjective orientation);
3. Experience alternate subjectivities[1] from a different ontological threshold produced by an open/plural hermeneutic framework for meaning-making (Identity shifting).

Dialogic practices developed in this book for the aforementioned objectives are expected to help students look inwards and critically analyze their own conceptual structures of arguments in their interactions with the religious other during class activities. This will help them address how their subjective identities influence their classroom participation and their attitude toward the religious other. It will also open up a hermeneutical gap—a discursive space, where students can reconstruct meanings and expand their interpretive matrix. In what follows, we delineate the dialogic practices developed to address each objective listed in this section.

---

[1] Though identity shifting has been identified as one of the most important dialogic practices of engagement under the third dimension of the counter-conduct framework developed in this book, it unfolds into and informs the fourth dimension of the framework i.e., experiencing a shift in subjectivities.

Identity in Dialogue: Creating New Social Identities in Dialogue with the "Other"

According to many scholars (Rojas-Drummond et al. 2006; Wegerif 2007; Wegerif and Mercer 2000) when young students are not introduced to dialogic practices of engagement, they often participate in "disputational talk" reflecting a fairly narrow sense of "self in dialogue" (Wegerif 2007). In this, students define their identity as opposed to the other such that their identity is strengthened only when they are able to dismiss and suppress other voices and ways of being. In the school, for instance, religious identities are created in a world of manichean binaries where the articulation of one identity depends on suppressing and marginalizing the other. During classes, students create project teams based on their religious identities and compete not only to earn grade points but also to establish the superiority of their religious community. In situating themselves as competent students, they first identify as loyal religious subjects and reinforce their allegiance to a particular religious community. Class projects, therefore, were used as a means to reactivate sentiments of religious animosity and enact practices of micro-aggression. This is what has been defined by Wegerif (2007) as the narrowly constructed sense of the "self in the dialogue."

In the school we worked at, students have narrow identity commitments that are fulfilled by expressing hatred toward the religious other. Identification with one's religious community is communicated by showing utter disrespect for differences that stand personified in the body of the religious "delinquent" who reifies an alternate set of practices. The problem with such engagement is that it creates a hostile and competitive discursive environment that mutes alternate voices from being heard over the dominant meta-narrative of religious hatred. In order to destabilize the hierarchy of interpretations and re-orient students toward acknowledging their stake and power in the meaning-making process, it is crucial to help them identify their biases and operate from the margins of their lived experiences. This can be done if students are taught to shift their focus from identifying with their self [religious identity] to identifying more with the dialogue itself.

For this, we decided to use media technologies as a dialogic space where students were involved more with the technology, i.e., with the dialogue on how to use the technology and less with their subjective identities. We organized "Training in Media Technologies" workshops for the students every week where they were taught how to use a DSLR camera, how to use a mobile phone, and how to produce shows for radio. Each workgroup included both Hindu and Muslim students who participated in activities centered around the use of media technologies. Groups were asked to draft a set of ground rules that would guide their conduct during the projects assigned to them. Each group member was asked to frame two rules of engagement which would apply to all the members in the group. Every member had the right to question or challenge the validity of each rule proposed so that the groups could create a list of "shared ground rules" for their group interactions. Many scholars (Barnes and Todd 1978; Littleton et al. 2005; Mercer 2000; Wegerif 2007) suggest that this dialogic practice of sharing the authorial role in drafting rules of conduct plays an important role in creating a truly democratic space of engagement because each member feels equally involved and responsible for upholding the sanctity of the dialogic space thus created. Some of the rules drafted by the groups have been enlisted in Table 5.1.

When students engaged in a systematic dialogue and focused on the technology in question, they were excited to establish their identity as "someone who is technologically advanced" by proactively learning how to operate/use the technological equipment. In activities where their social identities were not challenged or questioned, they experienced less threat from the religious other and were more open to seeking and giving help. Students sought help from those who were quick to learn how to operate the camera and were able to capture good photographs. In seeking help, they were willing to listen, share their discursive space with others and reinvigorate their interpretive matrix with new meanings and experiences.

We designed training tasks for them (Table 5.2), which encouraged them to think together and work toward solving problems.

Table 5.1 Shared ground rules

Sr. No.	Rules
1	All relevant information will be shared
2	Each member will be given 2 minutes to express his/her ideas
3	Each member will get a chance to question the ideas presented
4	Every alternative will be discussed before a decision is taken
5	The entire group will take the responsibility of the decision taken
6	Every member will be addressed respectfully and treated as an equal stakeholder in the process

Table 5.2 List of training tasks

Sr. No.	Group task
1	Use the camera assigned to you for the day to identify natural frames in your village and capture them esthetically
2	Use the recorder in the mobile phone assigned to you for a day to create radio content describing a day in your village
3	Use the camera assigned to you for a day to capture the essence of light in your village
4	Use the recorder assigned to you for the day to capture the natural sounds in your village

When the groups were given these assignments, students focused on devising a plan to execute the task and produce content. For instance, a group who was assigned the task of capturing the essence of light in their village had five group members—two Hindu students (Ajay and Mala) and three Muslim students (Rehana, Farhaan, and Aashiyana). The Hindu and Muslim students in this group had never interacted with each other in the school and when they were supposed to work together, their discomfort was evident in the initial stages. Before they were given access to the technology, Ajay and Mala sat separately in one corner while the other three members sat together to create a schedule and plan the day.

As soon as the group was handed the camera, Ajay took the lead and started engaging with the technology. He helped his group members understand the features of a DSLR and suggested that they should consider clicking photographs during sunset or sunrise as it is the best time to capture shadows. Given under is an extract from the transcript of the conversation between members of this group:

> *Ajay (a Hindu student)*: Why don't we click photos during the sunset? All will be free then?
> *Rehana (a Muslim student)*: My parents don't allow me to leave the house after 5 pm. I won't be able to come.
> *Ajay*: You can't always make excuses. Work is important. Also, the light will be very good for capturing light and shadows. Why don't you try talking to your parents? We can wait for a day?
> *Rehana*: But... they won't allow.
> *Aashiyana (a Muslim student)*: Rehana, you should try. Ajay is right. We can also capture the sunset if this plan works out. Ajay knows how to play around with the aperture. Ours will be the best photograph.
> *Rehana*: Ok!

Three things were clear from an analysis of this conversation. First, students acknowledged the expertise of Ajay and allowed him to lead the discussion. Students, in this project, learnt to identify more with the dialogue and less with their primary identity dimensions. Ajay's contribution was acknowledged because he had the technical skills required to execute this project. Second, Ajay was inclined to convince his group members to work together so that the team could submit a well-captured photograph. This signals the need to transcend communication barriers imposed by their primary [religious] identity in order to work together and produce results. Finally, when Aashiyana tried to logically reason with Rehana supporting Ajay's argument, it reflected how students can learn to temporarily suspend their religious identities/differences in favor of their curiosity to learn a new technology and engage in the dialogue (Image 5.1).

Implicit in this instance is a change in identity commitment that translates into a change in the relationship between students working together on a project. When students focus on the need to engage in an "exploratory talk" to solve the problem at hand, there is a marked shift in the way they relate to others in their group. Exploratory talk, according to many scholars (Littleton et al. 2005; Sams et al. 2005), promotes the use of reason wherein group dynamics are regulated by "shared ground rules" collectively drafted by the group members. Most of the groups that chose to follow the ground rules and focus on the dialogue and the process of meaning-making were able to submit photographs that precisely demonstrated the theme they selected. It was also observed that members of groups who were successful in submitting their media narratives on time were also more comfortable with listening to others, admitting that they were wrong, and changing their decisions in consultation with others.

When students engage in a systematic and exploratory talk, more often than not, a person who is more skilled and reasonable and who creates space for everyone to speak and contribute assumes the position of the group leader. This group leader plays a crucial role in changing the way one member relates to the other. Let us look at a conversation between six group members who were creating a plan to capture photographs of natural frames in their village.

Ruksaar (Muslim student): Let us start from the school? The broken window in the semi-demolished building in the playground can be a natural frame?
Mohin (Muslim student): That is not a natural frame? Why are girls so dumb! That is a man-made frame?

Image 5.1 Photo entry submitted by the group to illustrate the essence of light

Puja (Hindu student): You are breaking the shared ground rules by using derogatory terms and phrases for her. We can choose to ask you to leave the group if you continue being disrespectful.

Mohin (Muslim student): I am sorry (turning his face away from the group discussion). I still think that is not a natural frame.

Puja (Hindu student): Mohin, I think we are supposed to look for naturally occurring frames and not frames created by nature! Remember when ma'am gave examples which included a hole in the wall, a tunnel, or looking out of the door where the door becomes a frame?

Ruksaar (Muslim student): Exactly! A broken window can be categorized as a naturally occurring frame. You haven't created it, have you Mohin? (in a condescending tone).

Puja (Hindu student): Oye... (reprimanding Ruksaar)

In this conversation, Puja demonstrates a fair understanding of the shared ground rules and takes the lead in reinforcing them during group interactions. Also, she has a better grasp of the concepts taught to them in the "Training in Media Technologies" workshop. Other members, therefore, give heed to what she suggests as she tries to create a more open space for dialogue and deliberation. When Puja intervenes and puts forth her argument convincing Mohin to stick to the shared ground rules and also reprimands Ruksar when she misbehaves, she indicates a change in the relationship between the group members who are now guided by a sense of solidarity brought into play by the common code of conduct. This change in the relationship alters the way students address each other and relate to one another. Words that reflect a sense of care, cooperation, solidarity, and belongingness were exchanged between Hindu and Muslim group members in the course of the sessions. Some of the most frequently used words and phrases in these conversations that reflect an ethic of care include "sorry," "thank you," "he/she has a point," "let's stick to the rules," "let's listen," "give him/her a chance to speak," and most importantly "I was wrong." These words reflect the theoretical tenets of Robert Alexy and Julian Rivers's "Rules of Reason" (1990) according to which flexible social rules for dialogue create an ideal speech situation wherein individuals learn to reason by responding and recognizing needs of the other as they work together toward a common goal/purpose.

When students experience a change in the way they relate to one another, they enter a dialogic space where their engagements with the religious other are markedly different from the interactions they had earlier with each other in their community spaces including the classroom.

Intersubjective Orientation: Analyzing How Reimagining Conditions of Possibility Can Create Fissures in Subjective Identities

According to Bakhtin (1986), the opening of a dialogue always suggests the potentiality of the prevailing differences to generate new meanings and discursive possibilities. The process of meaning-making is embedded in the act of choosing one possible discursive relation over multiple others which exist in the same dialogic space. The presence of multiple possibilities of interpreting, meaning-making, referring to and associating with the other implies that any dialogue "always already" opens the possibility for a different meaning. Many dialogic theorists (Bourne 2003; Wegerif et al. 2005; Wenger 1999) who work in the field of education elaborate this concept to suggest that the way we engage with others and make sense of our social realities is mutually constructed out of a kind of dialogue. If we change the dialogue and explore social realities from the position of "dispossession" of one's primary identities (MerLeau-Ponty 1964), there is a possibility of reimagining the other by accrediting personal experiences with the other as a priori condition for meaning-making.

The process of "dispossession," according to Merleau-Ponty (1964), is the act of suspending the interpretive frame from which the self is perceived and conducted in relation to the [religious] other. The concepts such as "dispossession" or "identifying with non-identity" can be translated into theoretical principles which have implications for how students experience the religious other in and through the dialogic spaces they inhabit. Students can be encouraged to occupy a dialogic position of intersubjective orientation where they engage with a set of social issues pertinent to their lived realities and draw from each other's experiences. According to Kanpol (1992), critical pedagogies, therefore, must privilege the ideal of differences and reject a totalization of subjectivity based on religious identities. Students should learn to meditate upon the cultural sides of discourse production and reflect upon the rhizome of existing social realities and power relations which warrant their constitution as religious subjects by the way of ongoing dialogues with the religious other who is otherwise always excluded and invisibilized in their regimes of knowledge. Media educators can help students occupy such intersubjective positions. This process is divided into two phases:

Phase I

In the first phase of this process, we introduced students to the practice of developing "conceptual maps" and asked them to delineate perceptual nodes in their interpretive frame. Here, perceptual nodes refer to various mediated and non-mediated channels in their communicative ecologies, including organizations and individuals, through which they are introduced to the idea of a religious "other." This delineation allowed them to access the other in terms of who they are, what are their preferences, what are their life choices, and what are their roles in the society. Let us look at some of the conceptual maps created by students of grade seven; we have translated these from Gujarati to English.

Hussain created the conceptual map illustrated in Image 5.2 to represent

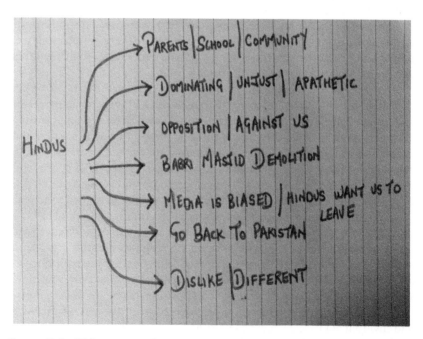

Image 5.2 This conceptual map was created by Hussain, a Muslim student in grade seven, before I started conducting sessions on dialogic practices of engagement in the school. This map represents Hussain's initial, uncritical perceptions of the religious "other"

his understanding of the religious other. This is the first phase of generating a hermeneutical gap where students create visual schemata of their interpretive frame and try to analyze how they come to see, perceive, relate to, and address the other. In this case, for example, Hussain was able to establish the boundaries of the conditions of possibility from within which the religious other is accessed and experienced. In doing this, students may recognize the limits imposed on their understanding by pre-given frames of references.

We probed Hussain further to help him read into his subjectification and analyze the influence of macro-institutions of power in the way he perceives the world. Also, this probing was an attempt to enable him to chart the power relations existing in his society and in the process demystify them by revealing the constructedness embedded in this naturally occurring power–knowledge complex. Given under is an extract from the transcript of the conversation that ensued between Hussain and the media educators.

Media Educator: Hussain, can you explain this conceptual map at length?

Hussain: hmm... I don't remember how and when I started understanding the difference between Muslims and Hindus. It seems as if I always knew that they were different from us. My *ami [mother]* used to scold us when we went to play with Ramesh in the *Thakur nivas.* Also, the *maulvi* in the *masjid* used to deliver lectures on how we are the descendants of one true God and those who do not follow the Quranic doctrines are doomed for eternity.

Media Educator: What were your experiences of playing with your Hindu classmates in the *Thakor niwas* when you were young?

Hussain: I don't remember...

Media Educator: Did you experience any form of hostility.

Hussain: To be honest, no... Ramesh and I still talk once in a while but now we are old and we have to act like adults.

Media Educator: What does that mean?

Hussain: I think we are now expected to follow our community rules; we can't make silly mistakes. Also, I like being a part of my community. There are things only we know—there are so many similarities between members of the same community. Also, when we do so many things together we get to spend more time with each other.

Media Educator: And who creates these rules—parents, community members or religious leaders?

Hussain (laughing): I don't know. I never thought about it. I think the rules *always* existed.

Media Educator: Do you think these rules can be changed?

Hussain: These are not some written rules that can be re-written. They are everywhere... You can't change everyone, right? Also, they are meant to maintain some order in our village.

During the course of this conversation, our goal was to help Hussain de-archive the origins of the rules prevailing in his society. The practice of apprehending a lack of certainty in how, why, and when a discourse emerges in a society is sustained by its members and is reinforced through everyday practices. This renders the universality of truth claims open to contestation and critical questioning. This was established when Hussain approached us the next day and said, "Ma'am, I asked my father about who created these rules in the evening yesterday. According to him, all these rules are mentioned in the Quran and well-read scholars such as the *maulvi* interpret it for us. All we have to do is have faith and follow them." There was a triumphant smile on his face. He was able to resolve the state of tension and uncertainty we had pushed him into. So we asked him yet another question, "Can the interpretations change if the *maulvi* changes? For instance, each student in this class submits a different and novel media narrative for the same theme because everyone thinks differently. Similarly, can the Quranic tenets mean something else if the *maulvi* has had different experiences in his life?" He looked at me for a long time and said, "I don't know."

Probing, therefore, is a dialogic practice which requires patience and critical skills. Based on the theory of dialogism and our teaching experiences, we devised three principles of probing students to elicit from them responses that enable a negotiation of meaning:

1. Each question must introduce an alternate perspective which would reveal the infinite chain of possible interpretations (Rommetveit 1992).
2. Each question must be an experience in a "shift in the identity" (Wenger 1999), i.e., the quest to answer the question must direct students toward an intersubjective orientation where interpreting social realities from a different position becomes crucial.
3. Each question must enable students to reject interpretive frames of dualism by introducing multiple voices in the text (Lave and Wenger 1991).

In our research experiences as media educators, these principles of probing students foregrounds in critical questioning skills and enables them to connect with the process of thinking as an end in itself. As Hussain explains, "Now I think that the answer is in the question you ask, no? This makes me realise that questions guide answers (laughing). If we change the questions, the answers will change. It is, therefore, very important to ask the right questions."

This is the moment—a resistive, counter-conduct moment—where media educators have to intervene and create a set of novel experiences for students that will allow them to engage and access their social realities from a different interpretive threshold. This is where the second phase of generating a "hermeneutical gap" sets in. In this phase, students were made to work on different media education projects in teams consisting of both Hindu and Muslim students. The objective was twofold: First, to produce new conditions of possibilities, i.e., new ways of engaging with the religious other and new ways of being; second, to create alternate spaces of conduct where students can experiment with their newly formed social identities (discussed in the previous section).

Phase II
The second phase of creating a "hermeneutical gap" starts right after the students have had the experience of working together on various projects. In this phase, we redistributed the conceptual maps submitted by the students in the beginning of the project and asked them to redraw these to include new perceptual nodes that emerged during the course of their interactions with their classmates. This helped them trace the change in their structures of knowledge and the way they think as they come to identify more with the dialogue and less with their primary social identities. According to Jonassen et al. (1998),

> The purpose of semantic networks is to represent the structure of knowledge that someone has constructed. So, creating semantic networks requires learners to analyze the structural relationships among the content they are studying. By comparing semantic networks created at different points in time, they can also be used as evaluation tools for assessing changes in thinking by learners.

When students looked at the maps they had submitted earlier, they looked a little amused. Some students tried very hard to convince us that we should allow them to discard the initial map and draw new ones. We, however, asked them to preserve the conceptual maps submitted earlier and modify them to include new perceptual nodes because we wanted them to trace the trajectory of their learning and evaluate the role of dialogic practices for collaboration in creating more inclusive classrooms. Let us look at the conceptual maps[2] submitted by Razina, a grade eight student (Image 5.3).

In the revised version of the concept map (Image 5.4), school emerges as an important perceptual node in the way Razina thinks about and experiences the religious other. She explains, "Talking with people who are different is important if we wish to work together. As we can't do that in our village, classrooms are the only safe places where such exchanges can take place. In the class, people talk about the work at hand and are able to collaborate regardless of their [social] differences." In collaborative

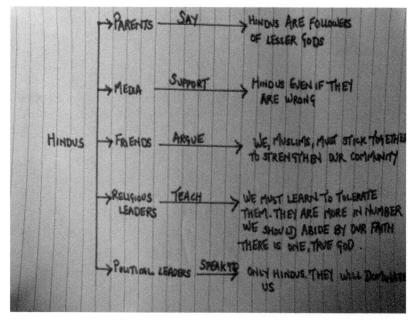

Image 5.3   Concept map submitted before the project started

[2]Students had created these conceptual notes in Gujarati language. We translated it into English while transcribing.

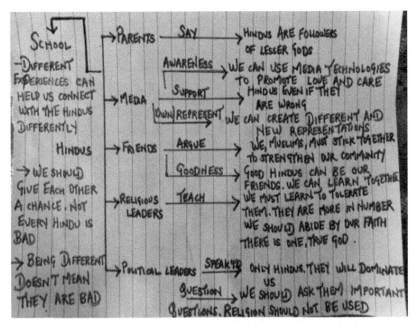

Image 5.4 Concept map submitted after participating in the sessions on dialogic practices of engagement. The revisions are highlighted through the use of a green sketch pen (Color figure online)

projects where engaging in the dialogue is the focus, new social identities emerge which help students connect with and care for one another as teammates. Also, these newly shaped social identities that draw from personal experiences foster an ethic of care in the classes and percolates into their everyday social realities when they rely on their critical thinking skills and dialogic engagement practices to analyze the influence of various other perceptual nodes in their meaning-making frames. Many students, both Hindu and Muslim, like Razina, for instance, realized their stake in the meaning-making process and decided to question the universality of the representations circulating in their society by creating new and alternative media narratives. From the revised conceptual map, it is clear that Razina assumes the responsibility and authority of authoring new and alternate representations of her Hindu classmates using media technologies. She comes to engage effectively with the potential of media technologies and use them to create tension in her own interpretive frame by juxtaposing her positive experiences against the socially circulated perceptions of the religious other. Arguing in favor of such classroom experiences of collaborative learning using dialogic practices of engagement, Sparsh, a Hindu student, said,

> Initially it is difficult. We know nothing about each other so it takes time to open up and come to like each other but once that happens conversations become smooth and easy. I enjoyed working on interesting projects with my classmates with whom I have never interacted before. Also, we got an opportunity to visit all the *dargahs* in the village during the photo walks. We wouldn't have done it on our own…also, we wouldn't have been allowed to visit these places. I, however, feel that this is temporary. As soon as we go back to our villages we start behaving as strangers again. This experience was different but I don't think we will be allowed to do so outside the classrooms. It will stay with us, nonetheless, and we can try to be more co-operative with each other.

What Sparsh has to say reflects that it is very difficult to bring about a change in the core identity of students in terms of a shift in attitude, thinking, and behavior witnessed in their everyday realities. A shift in their core identities can only be actuated by the way of sustained, long-term efforts in which educators and researchers should engage with the students and their communities. Such immersions must be designed to encourage parents and other community members to participate in this process if we are to ensure that students have access to environments beyond classroom spaces that are conducive to the practice of dialogic engagement and critical skills. Nonetheless, our observations and the testimonies of students, teachers, and parents alike indicate that the temporary suspension of primary social identities proves to be helpful in initiating students toward creatively considering experiential difference as a rational possibility. Students learn to engage with their own thought processes, ask relevant questions of the religious other, and develop a self-critical attitude which turns their gaze onto themselves and the socialization processes they receive.

A shift in identity can be conceived and experienced only to the extent that students are involved in intellection, i.e., the process of nourishing one's understanding with interpretations that stem from dialogic grounding of experiences. In this process, students resist the imposition of meanings determined by ideological sources outside the self (Giroux 1987,

1992). This doesn't, in any way, translate into students denying their self-identity, i.e., their predetermined religious identities. On the contrary, a shift in identity begins when students acknowledge that they enter a classroom with a bag of memories, relations, experiences, and feelings that give them a distinctive voice and character and an uncritical reliance on this acquired subject position may result in them being enslaved to live through the desires and expectations of the system.

The origins of this approach can be traced back to the works of several critical pedagogy theorists such as Freire (1970), Giroux (1988), Kanpol (1992), McLaren (1995), and Smyth (1987). This approach encourages media educators to subvert the "commonizing rituals" through which schools exculpate conformist intellectual behavior in favor of dialogic practices designed to gravitate students toward a critical self- analysis. In this moment of resistance, students experience autonomy, identity, and agency as they try to destabilize the established forms of conduct (Blühdorn 2006). This experience of a shift in subjective identities is the fourth dimension of the counter-conduct framework.

According to this dimension, as students experience alternate subjectivities they require a platform to enact/act out their newly acquired identities. Many media education scholars and activitists (O'Neill 2004; St John 2008) suggest that theater can be appropriated for creating a new reality and a new set of experiences in and through a story to subvert particular forms of action. This is because theatrical performance in critical media education is used as a strategy to produce a performing body that can defamiliarize itself from the assemblage of power relations in its community in order to recognize its previous lack of awareness. It is based on the principle of "time-space distantiation" which allows young students to use the stage as an abyss distancing them from their lived experiences. When students write/conceive or enact the role of the religious other, the dominant rationality is disturbed, their subjectification is challenged and they are encouraged to study the coalition of multiple contexts in which the performance was conceived and enacted. This helps them withdraw, if only momentarily, from the dominant practices of conduct in their communities as they immerse in the identity of the character being represented through them. Theater, therefore, is a critical media education practice that motivates students to access alterity in and through their bodies as they plunge into the character from the play. This involves critical reflection on the ways in which the character faces problems because of discrimination in the society, challenges the power relations, and finds solutions to the existing problems.

Drawing on all the conventions of conduct in real life, a theatrical performance was directed and staged over the course of this project in collaboration with students who occupied creative and authorial positions in the process. Theater was used as a means to dislodge the real-life state politics and create an induced experience of alterity. All the familiar categories such as Muslims, Hindus, religious leaders, community heads, *Panchatayat* leaders, teachers, and family members were performed but in a way that their performance entailed a change and the boundaries of each were transgressed as normal social identities were reinvented (Casquete 2006).

Experiencing Change in Subjective Identities: Theater as a Mode of Active Engagement

Many media education scholars such as Drotner (2008), Jenkins et al. (2006), Gee (2003), Henderson (2009), and others address how mediated spaces, especially online platforms, provide young people with the opportunity to adopt fictive identities and in the process develop a richer understanding of the "self in the world." According to these scholars, the use of theater or a performance space to interrogate one's subjective identities relies on the dialogic principle that any and each text (experience, social issue, reality, or other dimension of the material culture) is inexhaustible in that the existing/dominant interpretations can be appropriated, reshaped, and rearticulated in the course of new experiences that reveal new meanings of being and relating. Theatrical performances allow students to enter an eclectic zone where the purposeful integration of disparate elements and identities is possible (Garlough 2008). Participating in theater is a mode of active engagement, "one that encourages experimentation and risk-taking" (Jenkins et al. 2006). In this process, the disparate elements populate the same dialogic space but do not seek a resolution or synthesis. In other words, internal contradictions are accepted as given while participants (actors and audience) leave the predefined structures of conduct temporarily and disinhibit their minds to restage a performance of an alternate self in and through the fictional characters created. Through such experiences, students can adopt new fictive identities as they enter their roles in the play. This process helps them develop critical skills to evaluate and solve problems from multiple viewpoints, enter/exit regimes of knowledge other than their own to assimilate information, to redefine relations, re-appropriate core cultural practices, and alter relations with others on a mediated, fictional stage created by them.

In the next section, we explain why theater is a potential site for students to analyze and reshape their own situatedness in the world.

The Making and Doing of Theater: Performing Alternate Identities

In the villages, places such as the village lanes, community centers, places of worship, and other spaces act as mediated sites to forge social ties and develop communication. For young students in these villages, social realities and relations thrive in and are reified in the interaction between mediated and non-mediated experiences. In situations such as these, theatrical performances on streets, often referred to as *nukkad natak*, can provide an assemblage of people in close proximity for a conversation and act as a communication text where power relations are questioned and destabilized. Students work as authors and collectively produce a text that is translated into a lived experience of the alterity [alternate subjectivities] through performances. Several scholars (boyd 2007; Jenkins et al. 2016; Westheimer and Kahne 2004) suggest that this practice of self-designing realities for participation encourages young people to (re)create public and private spaces as they negotiate with and acknowledge the limits imposed by adult controlled real-life spaces (boyd 2007). In the process of creating a text, i.e., a play, where they are encouraged to share the authorship with others who come from different socio-cultural backgrounds, students encounter conflicting ideas and learn to negotiate with differences. The outcome of this often manifests in the form of a shared understanding of the cultural artifacts surfacing in the text produced at the end of the dialogic process of meaning-making. As students work toward the co-creation of a fictional world that challenges and questions the socio-political issues in their lived realities, they start reflecting from a dialogic position and take into consideration the disparate viewpoints which inform the nature of the spaces and their experiences with and in these sites.

To design a dialogic space for the production of theatrical performances, we formulated three principles based on the theories of critical media literacy and performance studies:

1. Principle of critical empathy: Critical empathy involves taking into consideration the other's perspective, entering a different realm of reality, and examining situations of discrimination from within the felt contours of the lived experiences of others (Valsamidis 2016). In this, students listen to others who constitute the performative space and relate with a plethora of experiences emerging out of diverse lived realities.

2. Principle of shared meaning-making: Here, a theatrical performance is conceived as a critical chronotope because it is dynamic; it is formed in the interaction of student's past experiences with their ongoing involvement in alternate realities as they draft "yet-to-be-accomplished" goals for themselves (Brown and Renshaw 2006).

3. Principle of intersubjectivity: In this, the producers, actors, and the audience all engage in scripting and re-scripting the play through participation before and during the enactments (Boal 1985). Performances, therefore, are dialogic and dynamic as they reflect not only the different voices within the text but also allow for interplay between the roles of the author and audience.

Students were encouraged to keep these principles in mind every time they sat down to write a script for the play. Acts of religious discrimination were identified as the exigency of the society that had to be addressed through various theatrical performances. Students in each class were divided into three mixed-religion groups: the scriptwriters, the directors, and the actors and each group followed informal guidelines to produce content. For instance, scriptwriters were supposed to select local issues from their community experiences that demanded critical attention and suggest ways in which these issues could be addressed through theatrical performances. Directors were responsible for executing the script, training/helping the actors, identifying places of performance, and ensuring that the execution of the script was such that it invited participation from the audience.

Finally, actors had to bear the onus of emoting the script so as to create a state of transience wherein both participants and audience could experience a friction in their subjective [religious] identities. Staging every theatrical performance, therefore, was a participatory process and emerged as an expression of the entire class community's "stories, issues, knowledge, and needs" (Prentki and Selman 2000).

During this production process, theater workshops were regularly conducted for students and they were introduced to the three main genres of drama, namely comedy, tragedy, and satire. Our observations revealed that students borrowed heavily from the popular culture scene and the local folk traditions. They were keen on using various folk elements and structures of narration/performance but wanted to infuse these with new contextual meanings to articulate social critiques. Also, according to them, using a familiar channel of communication invites greater participation from the audience as they are more comfortable to initiate an engagement in and through those familiar structures of narration and performance.

Besides the structure and language of the play, the space in which performances are staged serves an important role in either inviting participation or inhibiting it. In the village, streets are potential sites where children and adults exchange media texts and express their identities. Students, therefore, decided to use streets as a medium to initiate dialogues on routinized practices of religious discrimination in their villages and to increase the possibilities of participation from the community members.

Performance studies scholars such as Mason (1992) and Srampickal (1990) suggest that street plays remove the performative acts from the restraints of the predefined structures of theater building and situate them in the naturalized living environments of audience. As the performances move into the real-life spaces that people occupy, audience participation in the form of intervention during the performance or discussions toward the end of the plays seem more organic and accessible. According to Jaya, a Hindu resident of the village, street plays reduce the awe created around the act of staging a drama and bridges the gap between the performers and the audience. She says,

> If students would have asked me to leave my household work and go to the school to watch the play I wouldn't have done that. When they performed it right outside my house, I was compelled to step out and see what they were up to. Also, think about people who have never watched a play; they would never be confident walking into the school and participating in the discussion. When you bring a discussion to our homes we are more comfortable participating in it.

As is evident from this testimony, street plays engender a dialogic space at the intersection of the public and private spheres which allow for a unique exchange of ideas and experiences not available to many residents of the village. Several members, especially the women, who participated in such discussions, later declared that they were witnessing a street play for the first time and they never had had an opportunity to voice their opinions in a public forum before. Based on these observations, students produced street plays that allowed both the actor and the spectator to interchange their positions and critically engage in reimagining the contours of the social issue being addressed. This situates the actors and the audience in conversation with one another and exposes the friction inherent in addressing a social issue when it is experienced by different people in different ways.

Students producing street plays have to negotiate with new changes and suggestions recommended by the audience and in that they learn to pendulate between the varied subjectivities of their identities. In the production and performance of street plays lies the convergence of socio-cultural realities, material resources, representations, and narrative rituals through which students can advance social agendas and call for self-reflection and renewed identification (Howard 2005; Oring 2008; Sawin 2002). The vulnerability lodged in the very structure and content of this dialogic practice pushes students on the margins of their community engagement; they are required to reanalyze their socialization process, revisit their community interactions, and redefine their identities as they participate in the meaning-making process from within different roles (author, producer, actor, audience) and in relation to different people who are co-producers in this knowledge creation process. Street plays can prove to be an effective way to "act out" alternate identities publically and politicize the dominant socio-cultural forms in the society. In the next section, we discuss a play written and staged by students in their villages in order to elucidate these arguments and substantiate it with empirical data. The kernel of this exegesis is to demonstrate how theatrical performances can immerse students in orchestrated situations of alterity and generate a shift in their subjective identities.

Performing Alterity: Reinvestigating Practices of Religious Discrimination Through Satire

We now explain a play staged by students during the course of this program meant to address the dominant rationality of religious discrimination in the villages. In their play, titled Our Village, students wanted to focus on highlighting practices of discrimination prevalent in their village. They wanted to learn how to engage with their immediate socio-cultural contexts through theater and initiate a public debate in their community.

We realized that students could draw from culture jamming techniques to foment such debates through theatrical performances and so conducted workshops for them. The objective of these workshops was to equip students with production skills necessary for using media technologies alongside using satire to reveal the fault lines in their communities (Meikle 2007). Culture jammers emphasize that our experiences in the mediated world are dominated by multimodal texts and the only way to change this unprecedented influence of media representations in our lives is to appropriate the design methods/techniques from the mainstream popular culture scene to challenge the taken-for-granted representations in the contemporary culture (Kenway and Bullen 2008). Culture jamming, in the strictest theoretical sense possible, is a counter-conduct practice wherein the dominant semiological terrain is hijacked using the prevailing principles of media culture which sustain the popular culture scene. In this, the status quo is contested by a person who dwells in the community, i.e., is an insider, and is familiar with the regimes of truth and practices through which governmentality is reinforced.

Mark Dery (1993) calls this a kind of "semiological guerrilla warfare" used to not only provide radical commentary about everyday representations, but in doing so to subvert them and replace them with a counter form of representation/conduct that is more inclusive. Students used these tactics to produce another play, *Our Village*, and highlight the power–knowledge dynamics functional in their communities which reify the dominant rationality. They used popular songs from Bollywood film industry and rewrote the lyrics to create a satire on the practices of discrimination in the villages. The play starts with a song in Gujarati in which they describe their village in glorious terms. The lyrics are as under:

> Oh, let us tell you about our village!
> There is peace and prosperity in our village,
> Every problem finds a solution,
> Simple and clean living is our motto.
> Every morning the farmer visits his farms,
> He ploughs and works hard,
> We make manure from animal waste.
> In the evening, the school bell rings,
> All children run back home!
> In the night we all sit,
> Under the stars,
> Eat rotis made from bajra,
> And sleep with content in our hearts!
> This is our village, our life, our society!

Though the play begins at a point where students are painting a rosy picture of their village, their facade is immediately brought down as in the next scene a lady enters the stage and calls their lies by revealing practices of discrimination and hatred dominant in their village communities. The character of the lady is seen singing the following lines,

> Liar, oh Liar, let it now be, liar!
> Don't you know there is discrimination in your village on the basis of caste, language and religion.
> In your village the practice of untouchability is still upheld,
> People are punished for drinking and eating with others from a lower caste,
> Just because you speak a different tongue,
> You hate those who are not like you.
> You hate those who worship a different God!
> You may not say it, but you know this to be the truth…
> Tell me what is great about your village again…
> Tell me, Tell me…
> I won't be convinced by such false songs glorifying this village,
> Because,
> You are a liar, a liar, all of you are liars!

The tune of this song was borrowed from the popular Bollywood track *Kajra Re* from the movie *Bunty aur Bubli* and was rewritten to reference instances of discrimination in the village. According to Sahil, a member of the script-writing group, this was not only fun but also challenging at many levels. He explains,

> We wanted to be satirical and use references from mainstream media—popular songs to discuss issues which are socially relevant. Entertainment in media, these days, means people dancing and singing without a reason [satirically]. Our goal was to draw attention back to the powerful [transformative] role of a communication channel, a song, a performance, and emphasize on the different ways in which these very powerful technologies must be used. There is no denying that media should be and is used for entertainment but media can't be used "only" for entertainment. When we used these popular songs to discuss crucial issues which influence our everyday experiences, we bring back into focus a discussion about the role of media in the society.

They used popular songs as a literary trope to rope in the audience, increase their curiosity, and compel them to engage with the issue being discussed. When we asked them what techniques they used in the play to table a radical commentary on the social issue being addressed through this, Yash, another group member, said,

> Satire was used to create a state of discomfort among the audience members. Satire, as we discussed during the workshop, must make us feel uncomfortable and question our everyday experiences. If I feel like an outsider every time I enter a different neighbourhood, it reflects how unwelcoming [non-inclusive] we are; we pretend to lead a life where we tolerate others but that is a problem. We 'tolerate' them.

Students decided to stage this performance on the streets and invite village residents to stop them mid act and alter the narrative. This proved to be very entertaining for the residents and they started modifying the flow of the narrative. For instance, when an actor was singing the above-mentioned song and trying to highlight the problem of religious discrimination in the village, a Hindu resident intervened and said, "This is not true. We celebrate all the festivals together. Look at how we greet each other on Diwali and Eid. We are very inclusive." Another actor from the group of performers took to the stage to address this concern and asked the audience member if he had ever visited a Muslim's house for Eid or allowed his children to participate in the Eid-ul-Milad procession every year. The same question was then raised for Muslim residents who are cordial with their Hindu neighbors but never attend any of their family functions they are invited to. To this, a resident said, "It is not anyone's fault. We invite them and get invites in return but we all know it is just 'Talaf' (formality). Even they don't actually want to see us at their family functions." At this moment, students performing found a way to take the play ahead with the following song,

> This is not a problem specific to our village,
> The entire nation is suffering from this state of plight.
> Even if we know them, we don't make an effort to understand them.
>
> Media also strengthens this divide through biased representations,
> This is a game plan of people in power to stay in power.
>
> They are ruling in the name of religion,
> They are making us fight one another.
>
> I am worried because I know this is not progress,

I can see the long, dark night that awaits us all.

This song was composed to the tunes of the famous Bollywood track *Chinta ta Chita Chita* from the movie Rowdy Rathore. As soon as students started singing this song, the audience participated in the performance and expressed their enthusiasm by clapping and swaying to the music. This, however, doesn't imply that there was a transformation in the primary identities of either the children or the residents who were audience to the performances. Zabina, a Muslim resident from the village, argues,

> This looks progressive when performed on the stage but we will never see this change happen in real life. It is difficult to favor ideas which set you up against your community. If I allow my children to be friends with Hindus and I will be ostracized by my community. Also, why should I encourage my children to do such a thing when they are happy and content sticking around with their community members?

Based on our observations, we contest Zabina's argument and believe that performative practices and the experience of alterity help young students analyze their socialization process and re-identify with new groups formed on the basis of ideas of equality and work ethics. Theatrical performances help them enter unfamiliar regimes of knowledge and practices and allows them to think about an alternate form of engagement strategy that is more suited to diverse religious and social groups. Toward the end of this play, for instance, students included a scene wherein they suggest an alternate way of engaging with the "other", i.e., an alternate way of seeing the self in relation with the other. The lyrics of the song are as under:

> We live in a society full of differences,
> Difference in caste, creed, religion, language, and gender.
>
> We can't change the world,
> But we can change the way we see the 'other'.
>
> From shaking their hands in public,
> To recognizing their stake,
> From re-creating representations,
> To giving them a space,
> In being just to them,

We'll change our own selves.

I'd greet others with love,
And look beyond the boundaries of my religion and caste,
I will see them as one, as a Human,
And reimagine my role, as a Human, and not a religion or a caste!

We argue that students who use counter-conduct practices begin to operate in the registers of thought, and at the level of abstracting the now from the impositions of social identities and limitations. Theatrical performances which weave together multiple perspectives inaugurate a disinterested (unbiased) social inquiry into the prevailing dominant rationality and generate a "hermeneutical gap" in the interpretive frames of students by positing diverse regimes of knowledge in a shared, mediated, and experiential space for participation. The disinterested social inquiry, more often than not, reveals the fault lines (here, practices of religious discrimination) embedded in their communities and stirs a sense of discomfort toward their social identities. They are able to articulate their stake in reinforcing and reifying these practices and in the process generate new systems of conduct that allow multiple voices to manifest. Theatrical performances, in this sense, are third spaces that are created beyond the normalized routines followed by students in their communities and generate experiences for the participants that are completely detached from their lived realities.

Though students find it extremely difficult to create performative spaces for acting out and experiencing alterity in their lived realities, our observations reveal that the classroom space can provide the right environment for students to familiarize themselves with and enter new regimes of knowledge and practice. A classroom provides the required space to entertain differences such that we can delimit the social hierarchies that are naturalized in the minds of young students through primary socialization. Under the guidance of a media educator, classrooms can be infused with intended moments of creativity and fluidity which disclose alternative positions of "being" and equip young students with critical reflective dispositions to adopt and occupy these positions of otherness. No student will ever experience a complete detachment from their primary social identities due to any dialogic practice or critical education if the same principles of equality are not reiterated in the families and communities. Critical media education programs in schools, however, can equip students with the critical skills to ask the right questions and be able to transcend the boundaries of their uncritical religious identities. When students are given a chance to explore conditions of alterity in a safe and free space, they are excited to engage with the religious other and accomplish mutual goals as they rely on one another's strengths. We support and extend this line of argument because our observations reveal when students were asked to form work groups for projects toward the end of this media literacy program, they were keen on selecting their classmates who excelled at various tasks such as photography, acting, script writing, direction, and so on. When we asked Mehjabin, a Muslim girl student, why she insisted on working with her Hindu classmate Poonam for script writing, she said,

> I insist on working with her because she is very good at it and if we both work together our team is bound to put up a great performance. She has a keen interest in Gujarati literature and can play around with words. There are no doubts that we face limitations; we can't visit each other's house in the evening or after school and have to complete our work in the recess. Nonetheless, we enjoy working together and receiving rewards for our work.

Mehjabin and Poonam could never become close friends; they remained teammates for a long time but as soon as the projects were over, they stopped hanging out altogether. Nonetheless, they still have respect for each other which becomes evident during classroom discussions when they are ready to listen to the other even when their teammates don't wish to entertain a dialogue. Their experiences were reiterated by many other school students who are now more comfortable working in diverse groups and with students with different religious identities and lifestyles.

CONCLUSION

We deployed the counter-conduct framework to examine how religious politics govern the conduct of individuals. According to this counter-conduct framework, the conduct of individuals is disciplined in and through the regulation of the public sites they inhabit, the regimes of knowledge they draw from and participate in, the technologies of self-conduct they deploy to discipline the "self" in relation to the dominant rationality, and the everyday experiences they are immersed in. Given in Table 5.3 is a list of the four sites—both physical and discursive—through which the dominant rationality of religious discrimination is reified in the societies. Also delineated are the CML exercises developed to create a friction around the edges

Table 5.3 Counter-conduct framework for critical media literacy

Dimensions of governance	CML exercises	Objective	Evaluation	Outcome
Fields of visibility	1. Reimagining public spaces through **culture mapping** 2. Reimagining education sites through **body mapping** 3. Reimagining personal spaces by inserting the sites with the **"critical presence"** of the religious other	Work in inter-faith groups Co-create alternative media narratives Examine how the body is inscribed with religious markers by the virtue of its insertion into a public site regulated by religious politics Critically examine the rationality governing the religious segregation of public spaces Change the meaning of the exclusive spaces by occupying them in inter-faith groups	1. Analyzing photo-stories produced in inter-faith groups 2. Analyzing change in inter-faith group dynamics 3. Student testimonials/assessment reports	Students were willing to work in inter-faith groups because they wanted to own and use a media technology, i.e., camera Students co-occupied religiously segregated physical spaces Students assumed a sense of responsibility toward creating inclusive narratives in the authorial role

(continued)

Table 5.3 (continued)

Dimensions of governance	CML exercises	Objective	Evaluation	Outcome
Regimes of knowledge	1. Upsetting the rules of representation 2. De-neutralize systems of representations 3. Granting exclusionary authorship to a single religious community 4. Critically analyzing a short film engaging with the politics of representations	Encourage students to enter a stimulated experience of discrimination by asking the religious other to represent them based on the regimes of knowledge operational in the community of the other Encourage students to challenge this felt discrimination by initiating a collaboration with the author-cum-religious other Encourage students to access an alternative regime of knowledge and broaden their meaning-making system Encourage them to work as "bricoleurs" and upset the dominant trends circulated in and through the popular culture	1. Analyze the frustration among students when forced into situations of felt discrimination 2. Analyze how students negotiate with the religious other to create more inclusive narratives based on sharing in their regimes of knowledge 3. Compare the media narratives created when students worked in groups comprised of co-religionists with the media narratives they created when they worked in conversation with the religious other 4. Collect student and teacher testimonies 5. Prepare an observation schedule to classify the changes in the in-class dynamics during this activity in the role of a media educator	Students, who were encouraged to inhabit situations of felt discrimination, were keen to seek revenge in the beginning Later, they realized that producing equally biased narratives about the other didn't change the representations of their community in the classes Students decided to understand the life-world of the other before creating media representations of their community They were able to understand the politics and systems of regulations which inform the media representations of communities in a society They were equipped with technical skills to produce alternative narratives

Dimensions of governance	CML exercises	Objective	Evaluation	Outcome
Technology of (counter)conduct	1. Developing dialogic practices of engagement 2. Initiating "exploratory talk" around the use of media technologies 3. Creating shared ground rules for collectively regulating in-group dynamics 4. Generating a "hermeneutical gap" 5. Developing conceptual maps	To encourage students to widen their interpretive frames with meanings which emerge out of their interactions with the religious other To encourage students to create an inter-faith conversational realm wherein they can deliberate and engage with the everyday lived realities of the religious other and in doing this voice their experiences To enable students to recognize the broadening of their interpretive frame after sustained deliberation with the religious other Develop strategies to facilitate the smooth functioning of inter-faith teams To resolve differences in understanding and deliberation constructively	1. Observation notes delineating changes in affective intensities among students 2. Student submissions of conceptual maps tracing a change in their understanding of the "religious other" based on in-class experiences of working in inter-faith groups	Students were able to draft shared ground rules and this practice streamlined their in-group negotiations They were able to overcome initial reluctance of working in inter-faith groups when they realized in their dialogic engagement that the religious other was not necessarily bad They were able to examine the basis of their prejudice toward the religious other and try to change it They were able to observe the changes in their interpretive frame through the conceptual maps they created

(continued)

Table 5.3 (continued)

Dimensions of governance	CML exercises	Objective	Evaluation	Outcome
Change in subjective identities	1. Applied theater practices Script writing Directing Acting Producing Addressing audience critique	To equip students with a mediated site to experience alternative life-worlds and practice resistance To allow students to embrace new subjective identities and experience the complexities associated with those To create inclusive narratives To critique practices of discrimination in the villages and invite the residents to participate in this process through their engagement as audience members	1. Observation notes to understand the change in the affective intensities among students 2. Student assessment reports 3. Student testimonies 4. Parent/teacher testimonies	Students experienced a need to enter an alternative social realm of reality They were able to experience the discrimination felt by others and associated those with their own similar experiences In the mediated site and from within the imaginary character of the play, students were able to question the structures of power and dominance in their village communities Parents and village residents participated in this process of questioning the given by the virtue of acting as members of the audience group

of these sites of governance, thus challenging the practices and rationality concomitant with them.

Based on our experiences of working as media educators, we argue that critical media literacy programs in schools can provide young students with the skills required to challenge and/or upend the dominant discourse of religious violence, to create new narratives from the interstices, from the in between, and pendulate between the fixed identities subsumed in binaries such as self–other, victim–perpetrator, us–them, and most importantly in this case, Hindus–Muslims. Each exercise designed to address a particular social issue must be tailor-made to suit the local needs of the community and reference the lived realities of students, which makes this critical project extremely reflexive and iterative.

Throughout the course of this project, we continuously evaluated the effectiveness of the media education exercises designed, invited feedback from community members and participants, and involved students at all the levels of formulating the learning objectives and modules. In the next chapter, we provide a neat narrative delineating ways in which we evaluated the effectiveness of the exercises designed for the students. Also, we unpack the role of media educators who, in situations where discrimination is normalized, must constantly strive to create discomfort for students who operate from within the well-defined boundaries of familiarity and social identities. The media educator is identified as a trickster who induces friction in the taken-for-granted social structures without necessarily disrupting the authority (Velde 2012). We delineate how we accomplish this in our role of media educators as we operate on the margins of being an insider and an outsider simultaneously.

References

Alexy, R., & Rivers, J. (1990). *A theory of constitutional rights*. New York: Oxford University Press.

Bakhtin, M. (1986). *Speech genres and other late essays*. Austin: University of Texas.

Barnes, D., & Todd, F. (1978). *Communication and learning in small groups*. London: Routledge.

Blühdorn, I. (2006). Self-experience in the theme park of radical action? Social movements and political articulation in the late-modern condition. *European Journal of Social Theory, 9*(1), 23–42.

Boal, A. (1985). *Theatre of the oppressed*. New York: Theatre Communications Group.

Bourne, J. (2003). Vertical discourse: The role of the teacher in the transmission and acquisition of decontextualized language. *European Education Research Journal, 2*(4), 496–521.

boyd, H. (2007). Why youth (heart) social network sites: The role of networked publics in teenage social life. In D. Buckingham (Ed.), *MacArthur foundation series on digital learning—Youth, identity and digital media volume* (pp. 119–142). Cambridge: MIT Press.

Brown, R., & Renshaw, P. (2006). Positioning students as actors and authors: A chronotopic analysis of collaborative learning activities. *Mind, Culture, and Activity, 13*(3), 247–259.

Casquete, J. (2006). The power of demonstration. *Social Movement Studies, 5*(1), 45–60.

Dery, M. (1993). *Culture jamming: Hacking, slashing and sniping in the empire of signs* (Vol. 25). Westfield: Open Magazine Pamphlet Series.

Drotner, K. (2008). Leisure is hard work: Digital practices and future competencies. In D. Buckingham (Ed.), *Youth, identity and digital media* (pp. 167–184). Cambridge: MIT Press.

Foucault, M. (1973). *The birth of the clinic: An archaeology of medical perception.* London: Routledge.

Freire, P. (1970). *Pedagogy of the oppressed.* New Delhi: Penguin Books Ltd.

Garlough, C. (2008). On the political uses of folklore: Performance and grassroots feminist activism in India. *The Journal of American Folklore, 121*(480), 167–191.

Gee, J. (2003). *What video game have to teach us about learning and literacy.* New York: Palgrave Macmillan.

Giroux, H. (1987). Critical literacy and student experience: Donald Graves' approach to literacy. *Language Arts, 64*(2), 175–181.

Giroux, H. (1988). *Teachers as intellectuals: Toward a critical pedagogy of learning.* New York: Bergin and Garvey.

Giroux, H. A. (1992). *Border crossings: Cultural workers and the politics of education.* New York: Routledge.

Henderson, L. (2009, March). Let's all be neighbours on Will Wright Street. *Walrus Magazine,* 56–58.

Howard, R. (2005). A theory of vernacular rhetoric: The case of the "Sinner's Prayer" online. *Folklore, 116*(2), 172–188.

Jenkins, H., Clinton, K., Purushotma, R., Robinson, A., & Weigel, M. (2006). *Confronting the challenges of participatory culture.* New York: New York University Press.

Jenkins, H., Shresthova, S., Gamber-Thompson, L., Kligler-Vilenchik, N., & Zimmerman, A. (2016). *By any media necessary: The new youth activism.* New York, NY: New York University Press.

Jonassen, D., Carr, C., & Yueh, H. (1998). Computers as mindtools for engaging learners in critical thinking. *TechTrends, 43*(2), 24–32.

Kanpol, B. (1992). Postmodernism in education revisited: Similarities within differences and the democratic imaginary. *Educational Theory, 42*(2), 217–230.

Kenway, J., & Bullen, E. (2008). The global corporate curriculum and the young cyberflaneur as global citizen. In N. Dolby & F. Rizvi (Eds.), *Youth moves: Identities and education in global perspective* (pp. 17–32). New York: Routledge.

Lave, J., & Wenger, E. (1991). *Situated learning: Legitimate peripheral participation.* Cambridge: Cambridge University Press.

Linell, P. (1998). *Approaching dialogue: Talk, interaction and contexts in dialogic perspective.* Amsterdam: Benjamins.

Linell, P. (2003). *What is dialogism? Aspects and elements of a dialogical approach to language, communication and cognition.* Retrieved 31 December 2017 from http://www.tema.liu.se/tema-k/personal/perli/What-is-dialogism.pdf.

Littleton, K., Mercer, N., Dawes, L., Wegerif, R., Rowe, D., & Sams, C. (2005). Talking and thinking together at key stage 1. *Early Years: An International Journal of Research and Development, 25*(2), 67–182.

Mason, B. (1992). *Street theatre and other outdoor performance.* London, UK: Routledge.

McLaren, P. (1995). *Critical pedagogy and predatory culture: Oppositional politics in a postmodern era.* New York, NY: Routledge.

Meikle, G. (2007). Stop signs: An introduction to culture jamming. In K. Coyer, T. Dowmunt, & A. Fountain (Eds.), *The alternative media handbook* (pp. 166–179). London: Routledge.

Mercer, N. (2000). *Words and minds: How we use language to think together.* London: Routledge.

Merleau-Ponty, M. (1964). *The visible and the invisible* (C. Lefort, Ed. & A. Lingis, Trans.). Evanston: Northwestern University Press.

O'Neill, K. (2004). Transnational protest: States, circuses, and conflicts at the frontline of global politics. *International Studies Review, 6*(2), 233–251.

Oring, E. (2008). Legendary and the rhetoric of truth. *Journal of American Folklore, 121*(480), 127–166.

Prentki, T., & Selman, J. (2000). *Popular theatre in political culture: Britain and Canada in focus.* Bristol: Intellect Books.

Rojas-Drummond, S., Fernandez, M., Mazon, N., & Wegerif, R. (2006). Collaborative talk and creativity. *Teaching Thinking and Creativity, 1*(2), 84–94.

Rommetveit, R. (1992). Outlines of a dialogically based social-cognitive approach to human cognition and communication. In A. Wold (Ed.), *The dialogic alternative: Towards a theory of language and mind* (pp. 19–45). Oslo: Scandinavian Press.

Sams, C., Wegerif, R., Dawes, L., & Mercer, N. (2005). *Thinking together with ICT and primary mathematics: A continuing professional development pack.* London: SMILE Mathematics.

Sawin, P. (2002). Performance at the nexus of gender, power, and desire: Reconsidering Bauman's verbal art from the perspective of gendered subjectivity as performance. *Journal of American Folklore, 115*(455), 28–61.

Smyth, J. W. (1987). *A rationale for teachers' critical pedagogy: A handbook.* Melbourne, VIC, Australia: Deakin University.

Srampickal, J. (1990). *Voice to the voiceless.* New York: St. Martin.

St John, G. (2008). Protestival: Global days of action and carnivalized politics in the present. *Social Movement Studies, 7*(2), 167–190.

Valsamidis, P. (2016). Representing "Us"—Representing "Them": Visualizing racism in Greek primary school films. In J. Singh, P. Kerr, & E. Hamburger (Eds.), *Media and information literacy: Reinforcing human rights, countering radicalization and extremism* (pp. 213–222). Paris: UNESCO.

Velde, J. (2012). *From liminal to liminoid: Eminem's trickstering.* Bergen: University of Bergen.

Wegerif, R. (2007). *Dialogic education and teaching: Expanding the space of learning.* New York: Springer Sciences.

Wegerif, R., & Mercer, N. (2000). Language for thinking. In M. Cowie, D. Aalsvoort, & N. Mercer (Eds.), *New perspectives in collaborative learning.* Oxford: Elsevier.

Wegerif, R., Perez Linares, J., Rojas Drummond, S., Mercer, N., & Velez, M. (2005). Thinking together in the UK and Mexico: Transfer of an educational innovation. *Journal of Classroom Interaction, 40*(1), 199–211.

Wenger, E. (1999). *Communities of practice: Learning, meaning and identity.* Cambridge, UK: Cambridge University Press.

Westheimer, J., & Kahne, J. (2004). What kind of citizens? The politics of educating for democracy. *American Educational Research Journal, 41*(2), 237–269.

CHAPTER 6

Evaluating the Role of Critical Media Education in Mediating Counter-Conduct

Abstract In this chapter, we present a two-pronged approach we developed to evaluate the effectiveness of the media education exercises designed for and with the students. In the first phase, we analyze if there is a change in the way students negotiate and engage with media texts in and through the narratives they produced. This is done by describing situations of media teaching and media learning and is based on the observational notes of the media educator. The second phase, therefore, is characterized by new relationships and associations emerging during the course of the media education program, i.e., if there is a change in the way students relate to each other, do they use new, productive terms to refer to one another, and do they recognize the "other's" voice during group interactions. To corroborate a change in the attitude and relational affinity between students, we used testimonies submitted by teachers' and parents, self-reports of students, and our personal observational notes.

Keywords Evaluation techniques · Attitude change · Relational affinity · Role of media educator

© The Author(s) 2019   127
K. V. Bhatia and M. Pathak-Shelat, *Challenging Discriminatory Practices of Religious Socialization among Adolescents*,
https://doi.org/10.1007/978-3-030-29574-5_6

INTRODUCTION

Critical media education has for long been celebrated as a participatory process that is multifaceted and emphasizes the need to create learning opportunities based on the principles of collaboration and participation (Blythe
2002; Hobbs 1998, 2004; Kubey 2003; Stout 2002). In this project, media
education was deployed as a strategy to equip students with critical skills
necessary for working together and transcending the barriers imposed by
their primary social identities and their religious allegiance. This, we believe,
can give an impression that all the exercises designed to invite participation
were able to create a fraying around the edges of the dominant rationality
and inaugurate an emancipatory approach to educating young children. In
this chapter, therefore, we wish to rupture this utopian ideal of participation by acknowledging the "dark side" (Brookfield 1994; Reynolds 1999)
of critical pedagogy and suggest ways in which researchers can guide themselves against unintended dominance and control that they assert in their
roles as media educators.

In order to avoid the "social tyranny of participatory processes" (Ferreday et al. 2006), media educators must enact reflexivity at two levels. First,
media educators must ensure that critical media education exercises, in lieu
of promoting dialogic practices of engagement, do not result in prescribing
legitimate practices and perspectives in the classrooms. For this, students,
other teachers, and their community members must be included at various
levels of decision making. It is important for media educators to include
students in generating learning objectives, designing media education exercises, and analyzing the effectiveness of the steps taken. In this project, for
instance, it was crucial to allow students to enact their participation in various ways such as refusing to take part in classroom projects, expressing
their discomfort, or being reluctant to collaborate with students from the
other community to ensure their safety and well-being. The effectiveness
of media education exercises, therefore, was measured in the context of the
prevalent cultural and social realities in order to understand if and when this
project could make children "vulnerable" to the power structures operating
in their communities.

Evaluating media education exercises begins with incorporating not only
the self-reports of students, teachers' testimonies, and reports by parents
but also observation notes made by the media educators as they operate
from the margins of the community. This brings us to the next level where
reflexivity must be practiced, i.e., in articulating, enacting, and redefining

the role of a media educator in a project that strives to create tension in the dominant rationality. A media educator must be reflexive of what her presence entails for the students with regard to the friction it creates in the community.

In the following sections, we delineate a conceptual framework developed to evaluate the effectiveness of the media education exercises designed for and with the student and weave it with our observations as media educators.

EVALUATING CRITICAL MEDIA EDUCATION: DEVELOPING A COMPREHENSIVE ASSESSMENT METHOD

In this project, critical media education was used to develop a counter-conduct framework and challenge naturalized experiences of religious discrimination in the village communities. The objective of this framework was to help students understand how they are constituted as religious subjects by the macro-institutions of power, how they enact their subjectivity and reinforce the dominant rationality by participating in the everyday micro-politics of power, and how analyzing the origins of their subjective identities can encourage individuals to transcend these and develop alternate ways of being. In cases such as these, wherein critical media education can compel students to appropriate the center from the margins, they must be identified as vulnerable subjects who may not be aware of their stake in this process. Also, analyzing how effective these programs are in creating fissures in the dominant rationality can't be accomplished through a disinterested sociological inquiry that privileges the explicit shift in behavior or a quantitative statement of improvement in cognitive skills as a parameter of change over various implicit disruption in their subjective identities when they agree to work and collaborate with the religious other. Although some scholars illustrate the value addition created by quantitative data for assessing media education exercises (Erstad and Gilje 2008; Geiger 2001; Sun and Scharrer 2004), we argue that only using such evaluation tools fail to take into account the social complexities and cultural diversity in which students are embedded. According to several scholars such as Martens (2010) Fisherkeller (1999), and Scharrer (2006), it is easier to deploy quantitative assessment tools if the objective of the study is to evaluate the teaching of discrete facts. In other words, it is more difficult to evaluate the process of meaning-making, interpreting, asking critical questions, and producing alternate narratives using quantitative tools (Cheng 2009). How can we ascertain whether students have started using a critical inquiry-based method to generate content for media production activities? How can we measure the extent to which students have started to collaborate with each other, situating their opinions in conversation with the perspectives of the religious other in order to demystify the universality of truth claims? How can a media educator identify when and how students are rendered vulnerable to the threats of uncertainty if they learn to temporarily suspend their primary social identities, i.e., the religious subjectivities? How can we establish if a temporary suspension of primary identity allows students to envisage the need for proposing an alternate form of conduct in their communities?

Various scholars argue that critical media education assessment is a context driven endeavor (Potter 2004; Scharrer 2002) and must account for the various socio-cultural practices prevalent in the communities which influence their media engagement practices and the general nature of their communicative ecologies. According to Buckingham (2005), a generalizable assessment tool shouldn't be used to evaluate the effectiveness of media education exercises because such methods often favor specific readings of media messages as correct or socially validated, thus creating a hierarchy of understanding in the proposed structureless realm of the classroom. We wish to substantiate this line of argument with our research and assert the need to develop a reflexive and holistic approach suited to the socio-cultural contexts for which the projects are designed.

The focus of this research project is to enable children to acknowledge the limits of their socialization and in doing so to retrace their boundaries in relation to the new experiences and exposure to alternate regimes of truth and practice. This is with regard to their constitution as a religious subject which is a sensitive topic because attempts to address it exposes students to a multitude of possible threats from the village elders, community members, and religious leaders. In order to evaluate the effectiveness of the media education program, it is crucial for us to observe and account for the ways in which they learn to negotiate with these threats and limitations and continue to participate in classroom activities to assert their stake in the meaning-making process. Also, in this context, it was essential to recognize when and where students felt that they were being threatened due to the uncertainties they were exposed to. Though many students wanted to participate in the classroom activities, there were some who wished to reiterate their allegiance for their religious identity by perpetuating discriminatory practices in the class such as refusing to eat with the other, not giving due credit to a teammate/classmate because of their religious identity, or silencing members by ignoring their suggestions during classroom discussions. As media educators, we had to continuously modify media education exercises to include dimensions and experiences that made such students feel less threatened or challenged. The effectiveness of this approach could only be assessed on the basis of the changes we observed in the way students enacted their participation, the kinds of narratives they created, and the dialogues they inaugurated.

Based on available literature and our experiences as media educators, we developed a two-pronged approach to evaluate the effectiveness of the media education exercises designed for and with the students. In the first phase, we analyzed if there was a change in the way students negotiated and engaged with media texts in and through the narratives they produced. This was done by describing situations of media teaching and media learning and was based on the observational notes of the media educators. It included analyzing if students were able to comprehend the influence of power–knowledge complex and address it by creating alternate narratives. The second phase, therefore, is characterized by new relationships and associations emerging during the course of the media education program, i.e., if there is a change in the way students relate to each other, do they use new, positive terms to refer to one another, and do they appreciate the others' suggestions during group interactions. To corroborate a change in their attitude and the felt relational affinity between students, we used testimonies submitted by teachers' and parents, self-reports of students, and our personal observational notes. In the following sections, we elaborate on these two phases of assessing the media education program and corroborate it with testimonies submitted by students, teachers, and parents.

Phase I: Describing the Context—Media Teaching and Media Learning

According to many media education scholars such as Hart (2001), Hobbs (2004), and Scheibe (2004), there is a dearth of descriptive research conducted to study classroom teaching. These scholars argue in favor of the need to document everyday classroom interactions between teachers and students in their naturalistic setting using qualitative methods. They believe that such detailed accounts offer insights related to the how, why, and when of the media education activities conducted. Classroom-based research can yield rich insights into the relationship between students' communicative ecologies and the media education exercises designed for them, i.e., are they interested to participate, does challenging their truth claims threaten them, how do they negotiate with alternate regimes of knowledge and practices of conduct, and so on.

Drawing from this rich literature available in the field of media education and classroom studies, we developed a media education assessment framework to identify transversal competencies based on which the effectiveness of the exercises could be evaluated. The transversal competencies were divided into three types: Technical skills, critical comprehension, and openness to "differences."

1. Technical Skills: This includes analyzing if students have acquired the technical skills required to utilize a media technology. For this, students were given access to different media technologies such as camera, recorder, and mobile phones, and were introduced to the basic features of each of these technologies. They were encouraged to use the technology and submit media narratives such as photographs, short video films, or an audio file, illustrating their efficiency in the use of a media technology. Workshops were conducted at regular intervals to help students clarify their doubts and resource persons were invited to inaugurate them into the technique of creating a media story. For instance, students were introduced to the narrative structure of a news article and how to use the principle of inverted pyramid while drafting one, they were introduced to the basic features of DSLR such as the focal length, the aperture, the ISO and other settings, and instructed on how to use a camera to depict a particular idea, and so on. Their technical competencies were evaluated on the following parameters (Table 6.1).

2. Critical Comprehension: Critical comprehension is the ability to remove a text from the confines of its denoted meaning and posit it in the larger framework of the dominant rationality. It involves unearthing the political and ethical force in the creation of the text and its resultant implications. Students who can critically engage with a media text are able to discern the intentionality of the author(s) and trace/recognize its role in reinforcing or challenging the power–knowledge complex. They are also able to illustrate how the discursive field created by the circulation of media narratives engenders particular forms of conduct prevalent in their localities. We devised five parameters to evaluate if a media education exercise was able to foment critical comprehension skills in students (Table 6.2).

Table 6.1 Technical skills

Sr. No.	Parameters
1	Narrative structure: Is the media text well-constructed according to the principles of narrative succession? This includes analyzing if the transitions are seamless, if the narrative gives appropriate space to relevant dimensions of the story, if information is carefully filtered to avoid any factual errors and so on
2	Expertise in the use of a technology: Can the student explain why he/she has used a particular technique to create a narrative/story?
3	Expertise in editing skills: Is the student efficient in stitching the different strands of the story together to create a meaningful narrative? Can students use simple softwares such as *Movie Maker* and *Audacity* to produce consumable media texts?

Table 6.2 Critical comprehension

Sr. No.	Parameters
1	Identifying the intended audience: Can students understand who are the intended audience of the text?
2	Identifying the implicit meaning: Can students identify the main objective for creating a given text? Does the text indicate an inclination in favor of a particular ideology or perspective?
3	Challenging biased representations by producing alternate media texts that are more inclusive
4	Situating the text in the wider discursive field dominant in their communities: Can students relate a single narrative with larger socio-political issues pertinent to their village, state, and country?
5	Localizing the text to evaluate its influence on everyday realities: Can students identify how media narratives permeate their routines and influence their interactions with the religious other?

3. Openness to Differences: Media educators can analyze if media education programs encourage students to access alternate truth regimes and consider multiple perspectives. The effectiveness of a media education program can be evaluated on the basis that it creates a dialogic space where different voices are put in conversation with each other. The goal of a media education program that tries to address the social exigency of religious discrimination is to create inclusive, inquiry-based, learning experiences where students enjoy working together and collaborating over media production process. In order to assess if this media education program was able to initiate students

into engaging with differences, we deployed the following parameters (Table 6.3).

As is evident, in the first phase, we analyzed the effectiveness of the media education program on the basis of how proficient the students were on the competencies. Based on these parameters we analyzed how students negotiated and engaged with media texts in and through the narratives they produced. The various exercises that are demonstrated in the earlier chapters under each dimension of the counter-conduct framework are the final iterations and include various modifications that were introduced during the course of this program.

It is important to note here that the assessment of how effective a media education exercise/program is cannot be limited to analyzing students' engagement with the media texts in the form of either consumption or production. It is crucial that the influence of media education is analyzed in relation to its effect on their everyday interactions with the religious other. In the second phase, therefore, we designed the assessment to comprehend the changes in students' attitude, values, and behavior toward the religious other. We relied on testimonies submitted by parents and teachers, and self-reports by students to understand how and why a media education exercise was enabling them to converse with differences. In the following section, we delineate how we conducted assessment in the second phase where the focus was to attend to the change in relational dynamics between the students and to identify and/or mitigate the consequent threats posed by

Table 6.3   Openness to differences

Sr. No	Parameters
1	Including multiple voices: Are students willing to include voices representing varied socio-cultural contexts in the narratives they produce? For instance, in creating an audio tape recording natural sounds characterizing their neighborhood, are they willing to include sounds from diverse socio-cultural settings and varied village areas even if they don't frequent those places?
2	Analyzing the limitations of the narratives produced: Can students delineate the limitations imposed by their subject positions when they create a narrative? This is evident if they are able to accept that they have a limited understanding of a topic, are able to seek help from the religious other, or willing to share their authorial responsibilities such that the different voices find expression through the text

their communities. The second phase, therefore, exemplifies ways in which a media educator can assess a shift in the subjective identities of the students but also brings forth the politics of dominance ineluctable from practices of participation if the teacher doesn't attend to his/her limitations/biases and prejudices reflexively.

Phase II: Assessing Affective Relationality Between Students and Avoiding Pitfalls of Critical Praxis

In this phase, a media educator begins by appreciating the intrinsically disruptive nature of using critical praxis to reanalyze one's subjective identities and the disturbances it can cause in the lives of young students. We used self-reports submitted by students and corroborated those with our observations and testimonies from teachers and parents. For this, at the end of each month, we asked students to submit reports on what they had learnt. Similarly, we requested school teachers and parents to provide testimonies describing if they had noticed a change in the behavior of children in the school and their homes. Each child's progress was carefully monitored to understand if they were able to critically analyze their conduct in relation to the religious other as well as the self. To chart this progress, students were evaluated on the basis of three dimensions:

1. Values: Has there been a change in the way students relate to one another? Do they identify the other positively as co-learners?
2. Attitude: Has there been a change in the way students identify the other? Are they willing to work with students from the other religious community? Are they willing to listen to the other? Do they respect the shared ground rules created by their group?
3. Behavior: Do the students produce narratives that are inclusive and incorporate multiple voices? Do the students question the dominant forms of conduct in their communities?

Each student's progress was evaluated across these dimensions and a progress report was drafted at the end of every month. Based on our analysis of the change in the affective relationality among students, it was clear that students who had worked with us for three years were more reflective of their stake in the meaning-making process while creating media narratives than students who had spent less time participating in the media education exercises. Students who were involved at every step of this project generated media narratives that were more inclusive and representational. They learnt to effectively engage with the religious other, widen their interpretive matrix, and analyze mainstream media content critically. Not only were they critically aware of the interplay of power and knowledge in reinforcing the dominant rationality but also asserted their role in either challenging it or reifying it in and through their conduct.

As has been demonstrated, this project derives power from its ability to generate a dialogic space wherein students can imagine, desire, and act differently. It is crucial to acknowledge that such a participatory endeavor also puts them up against a powerful structure of governance supported by an entire community of "believers." Media educators need to be vigilant of and address the tension created in the lives of students who enact resistance, even in performing simple actions like participating in media education exercises that are designed to upend the dominant rationality and propose an alternate form of conduct. Students, by the virtue of participating in a media education exercise in the class, may expose themselves to contestations leveled at them by both their subjective identities (internal) and community members (external). For instance, many students who wanted to participate in theater activities and perform in front of an audience were not permitted to do so. Parents of these students, especially those of girl students, warned them against occupying public spaces (street as a stage) to voice opinions that might offend the elders in the villages.

Parents expressed their concerns through these testimonies and made us realize how students might either be enacting participation because they felt a sense of compulsion to do what others were doing. Sometimes, students had to argue with and challenge their parents at home to obtain their permission. In either of the cases, participation doesn't emerge as an emancipatory ideal because it creates an alternate hierarchy of opinions such that students who think and behave differently are alienated within their learning communities. Students may, thus, feign support in favor of opinions that are popular in the classroom. Scholars such as Brookfield (1994), Reynolds (1999), and Goldstein (2007) call this the "tyranny of participation." We used the four themes generated by Brookfield (1994) to recognize and exemplify the dark side of the critical praxis and participatory approach developed by this media education program: impostorship, roadrunning, need for community support, and cultural suicide. These are described and substantiated with testimonies submitted by students and parents as under:

1. Impostorship: When students feel that they lack the skills to partic-ipate in political discussions, they tend to withdraw and occupy the margins. This happens if the students are not aware of a political issue being discussed, fail to articulate their opinions, or feel overpow-ered by other members in their group. Komal, a class eight student, explains, "I don't generally read newspapers and my group members discuss political issues on a regular basis. They never make an effort to update me with what is happening. I always choose to remain silent because if I suggest anything they will make fun of me ... they will say that I can't express anything because I know nothing; but I live in the same village and have my experiences to share." In order to address this concern, a media educator must reflexively develop ways in which the activity of reading newspapers is not considered to be the most important quality for developing critical comprehension skills. We encouraged students to include media narratives circulating in and through the varied channels in their communicative ecologies includ-ing but not limited to what their parents/family members discuss at the dinner table, what their friends and peer circles relay to them, what they experience in their everyday interactions with the other, and so on.

2. Roadrunning: When students are introduced to new modes of think-ing, reading, and interpreting, they struggle in comprehending their engagement with media in particular and their routines in general. For instance, when students are recommended to juxtapose multiple media narratives while critically analyzing a political issue, they don't know how to make sense of this process. During the newspaper read-ing sessions, students didn't know how to enact their participation, approach the issue being discussed, or critically read the narrative pre-sented to them. For the first two sessions, only a very few students would participate and express their interpretations. We wanted to help students critically read the narrative and present their interpretation confidently. We, therefore, created an analysis sheet for them based on which they were supposed to break down their reading of the text. This analysis sheet required them to answer the following questions: Who said to whom, through which channel, in what ways? This was followed by asking them to sketch the expected/intended outcomes of a given text and provide strong reasons justifying their answers. This helped them identify a starting point in the course of critically reading a media text and they kept bringing in new creative moments

in the interpretation process as they gained confidence in enacting their participation.

3. Need for community support: Many students expressed opinions and ideas which they knew would be well-received by others in the learning communities. Some of the students, for instance, discussed the need to respect different religious communities during group and classroom discussions. They also created narratives which were inclusive of different perspectives and contributed toward sustaining a dialogic space in the classroom. These students, however, exhibited an altogether different worldview and very rigid political/social opinions as soon as they stepped out of their classrooms and into their primary religious communities. We were able to understand this tension between their enacted classroom identity and their primary social identity when we frequented their homes and interacted with them in non-formal, personal spaces. Let us take the example of Dharmesh, one such student in grade seven, who acted in accordance with the expectations of his group members in the class. He used to participate whole-heartedly in groups constituted by both Hindu and Muslim students and extend his support toward creating more inclusive spaces in the village. The online messages he circulated in his personal groups, however, were contradictory to his classroom rhetoric. His online messages talked about the threat imposed by the ever-growing Muslim community and urged all Hindu people to unite and fight the one true battle. We analyzed the self-report he submitted in which he states, "Not everybody likes working in a group. While you are working in a group, sometimes, you have to agree with what others are saying or else they will not include you in the decision-making process." Likewise, we observed some other students who supported popular opinions so that they were not excluded from the group. As media educators, it is very difficult for us to address this problem. Though we made an effort to create more democratic spaces in the classroom, we had no control over the student interactions that emerged in these spaces. In reflexively accounting for this limitation, we decided to create shared ground rules which allowed all students to express their opinions but it was difficult to convince students to express only that which they truly believed in. There are some experiences intrinsic to the constitution of their primary identities which can neither be altered nor erased. Also, some of these students refuse to contemplate the possibility of revisiting their interpretive frames

because they feel threatened by the influx of the multiplicity of new ideas. This fear that they will lose their culture if they accommodate differences is what defines the next theme.

4. Cultural Suicide: When students are put in a situation where the old hierarchies of social relations and governance are no longer valid, they find it challenging to grapple with the truth of a structureless realm that replaces old certainties. A young student from grade six once asked me, "Ma'am, if our God didn't create the world, who did? If my religion is not true, which religion is the right religion?" Media educators must attend to this feeling of uncertainty that stems from destabilizing their interpretive frames of meaning-making and analysis. Students must be convinced that questioning one's subjective identities is not directed toward a nihilistic state where no structure exists. Critical reflection as a form of counter-conduct must strive to give rise to an alternate form of conduct and meaning-making which is more just and inclusive. When they begin challenging their primary identities, it will take time for them to reach the next stage wherein they learn to associate with new social identities. The liminal phase between these two developmental stages is where a hermeneutical gap will be created in their discursive field and they will learn to add new references for and experiences with the religious other to their interpretive matrix. Also, media educators must pay special attention to the possibility that enacting resistance in the form challenging the dominant rationality in their villages may cause students to experience a sense of isolation and exclusion within their existing religious communities. To avoid this, media educators must adopt ways to involve the larger community (parents, teachers, and village elders) in all the activities designed for the students.

As has been illustrated, in our role as media educators we created learning conditions designed to distance our students from the established network of connections that influences their interactions in the cultural spaces of the village. As mentioned above, it was a challenging experience because some students felt a sense of dejection; they were offended when we compelled them to work together if they wanted to learn how to use the camera and the laptop. This often created an ethical conflict within us—Were we allowing our students to exercise their choice? Were we allowing them to believe in truth claims they had put their faith in? Were we subjecting them to some unintended harm by encouraging them to enact practices of resistance by working with children from the other religious community?

CONCLUSION

Media educators play a crucial role in identifying and working with the vulnerability inherent in such sensitive contexts. They must be ready to answer three crucial questions when they embark on a journey to create a sense of tension among young individuals with the intention of encouraging and enabling them to question power structures in their societies:

1. How do we account for our limitations and negotiate with our biases?

When media educators initiate a project/curriculum designed to question the lived realities and social hierarchies in a community, they should start with acknowledging their privileges and biases. As media educators, we created word clouds listing some of our several privileges—highly educated, urban residents, access to different forms of technologies and media texts, exposure to different cultures and societies, members of liberal families and communities, and so on. Doing this helped us in two ways:

a. We were able to realize that the ways in which we enact and experience forms of resistance vary from those who come from different socio-economic, cultural, and political backgrounds. In other words, for us, the simple practice of questioning and challenging our parents is a routine activity. Contrarily, students from these villages required assistance, teaching, and guidance to initiate them into questioning their parents during dinner conversations.

b. We were able to use our experiences as examples to delineate a realm of possible existence which was removed from their lived realities. We were able to help them imagine new ways of experiencing and enacting their roles as members in a society. What does it mean to work in environments wherein individual merit is more important than acquired social identities? What is their role and responsibility within the larger scheme of things we identify as India? What are the repercussions of creating and/or fostering hatred in one's neighborhood?

2. How do we respect the agency of young individuals?

When media educators work with young individuals, they often fail to step beyond their authoritative role as teachers. Young individuals require guidance to develop and practice critical competencies. This guidance must be limited to creating safe spaces where students can participate in alternative experiences of collaborating in inter-faith teams and working with people from different social backgrounds. This can be done when media educators begin from a place of respect for the students and their cultural values and/or beliefs. This doesn't mean the educators shouldn't try to help students recognize the inherent faults in their communities. The approach, however, must be embedded in a deep sense of respect and trust for each other. For instance, even when the media educators consider *Hijab* and *Burkha* as disciplining techniques used to control female bodies, they always respected their students' intention to use these as symbols to represent their religious beliefs.

3. How do we create a safe environment for young individuals to practice resistance?

Classrooms can and should be remodeled as safe contact zones where students can learn, question, challenge, and reimagine any text/experience. For this, media educators must create exercises to help students identify their potential as effective—critical authors/interpreters of the texts they read, create, and circulative. We have listed a few strategies we used to encourage our students to own the learning process:

a. Creative Liberty: After the initial training workshops, students were given media technologies to operate as they wished without any instructions on how they can and/or should use these technologies. For instance, when students were asked to create photo-stories, the educators refused to provide technical guidelines on what is considered to be a good photo. Once the photo-stories were submitted, the educators and students sat down together trying different angles, frames, contexts, colors, and so on to collectively decide which photo techniques produce the most telling and effective photo-story.

b. Dialogic Practices: Media educators encouraged students to think, conceptualize, frame, and ask relevant and critical questions in order to analyze media texts. Media educator's role was to facilitate discussions and inter-faith exchanges. They provided students with access to information, technologies, and other material resources while trying to encourage them to work and think together. Classrooms emerge as safe spaces when students and teachers learn to think together.

Based on our experiences, we argue that media educators must create spaces and experiences which allow people from different ideological chambers to cohabit and evolve in conversations with others. In times where media organizations and texts are creating echo chambers, the role of media educators is to develop learning strategies aimed at creating and nourishing conversations around religious discrimination, physical violence, and systemic othering reinforced in and through media. They need to design such experiences even in situations where it is challenging to host differences in the same space of learning.

It is crucial to realize that though we have focused on religion, the phenomenon of othering is practiced based on several other dimensions such as race, caste, gender, and class. The readers are, thus, encouraged to adapt our pedagogies to address their own concerns. It is important that young individuals are given opportunities to reflect upon their painful daily experiences of lived discrimination. Media educators can use classrooms and media texts as sites to draw these realities into learning spaces and engender critical discussions around them. Media educators can deploy critical media education as a carrier of unpublished realities that help individuals reimagine their lives together as is possible within discourses, experiences, and practices of inter-faith collaboration, critical engagement, and collective enrichment.

References

Blythe, T. (2002). Working hard for the money: A faith-based media literacy analysis of the top television dramas of 2000–2001. *Journal of Media & Religion, 1*(3), 139–151.

Brookfield, S. (1994). Tales from the dark side: A phenomenography of adult critical reflection. *International Journal of Lifelong Education, 13*(3), 203–218.

Buckingham, D. (2005). *The media literacy of children and young people: A review of literature on behalf of OFCOM* (Project Report). London, UK: OFCOM.

Cheng, K. (2009). The times they are a changing: Media education. In C. Cheung (Ed.), *Media education in Asia* (pp. 13–18). Dordrecht: Springer. https://doi.org/10.1007/978-1-4020-9529-0_5.

Erstad, O., & Gilje, Ø. (2008). Regaining impact: Media education and media literacy in a Norwegian context. *NORDICOM Review, 29*(2), 219–230.

Ferreday, D., Hodgson V., & Jones, C. (2006). Dialogue, language and identity: Critical issues for networked management learning. *Studies in Continuing Education, 28*(3), 223–239.

Fisherkeller, J. E. (1999). Learning about power and success: Young urban adolescents interpret TV culture. *Communication Review, 3*(3), 187–199.

Geiger, W. (2001). Talk about TV: Television viewers' interpersonal communication about programming. *Communication Reports, 14*(1), 49–59.

Goldstein, R. (2007). The perilous pitfalls of praxis: Critical pedagogy as "regime of truth". In R. Goldstein (Ed.), *Useful theory: Making critical education practical* (pp. 15–29). New York: Peter Lang.

Hart, A. (2001). Awkward practice: Teaching media in English. *Changing English, 8*(1), 65–81.

Hobbs, R. (1998). The seven great debates in the media literacy movement. *Journal of Communication, 48*(1), 16–32.

Hobbs, R. (2004). A review of school-based initiatives in media literacy education. *American Behavioral Scientist, 48*(1), 42–59.

Kubey, R. (2003). Why U.S. media education lags behind the rest of the English speaking world. *Television New Media, 4*(4), 351–370.

Martens, H. (2010). Evaluating media literacy education: Concepts, theories, and future directions. *Journal of Media Literacy Education, 2,* 1–22.

Potter, W. J. (2004). Argument for the need for a cognitive theory of media literacy. *American Behavioral Scientist, 48*(2), 266–272.

Reynolds, M. (1999). Grasping the nettle: Possibilities and pitfalls of a critical management pedagogy. *British Journal of Management, 10*(2), 171–184.

Scharrer, E. (2002). Making a case for media literacy in the curriculum: Outcomes and assessment. *Journal of Adolescent & Adult Literacy, 46*(4), 354–358.

Scharrer, E. (2006). Sixth graders take on television: Media literacy and critical attitudes of television violence. *Communication Research Reports, 22*(1), 325–333.

Scheibe, C. L. (2004). A deeper sense of literacy: Curriculum-driven approaches to media literacy in the K-12 classroom. *American Behavioral Scientist, 48*(1), 60–68.

Stout, D. A. (2002). Religious media literacy: Toward a research agenda. *Journal of Media & Religion, 1*(1), 49.

Sun, F., & Scharrer, E. (2004). Staying true to Disney: College students' resistance to criticism of The Little Mermaid. *Communication Review, 7*(1), 35–55.

References

Ahmed, S. (2010). The role of the media during communal riots in India: A study of the 1984 Sikh riots and the 2002 Gujarat riots. *Media Asia, 37*(2), 103–111.

Alexy, R., & Rivers, J. (1990). *A theory of constitutional rights.* New York: Oxford University Press.

Altheide, D. L. (1994). An ecology of communication: Toward a mapping of the effective environment. *The Sociological Quarterly, 35*(4), 665–683.

Amin, A. (2010). *Land of strangers.* Cambridge: Polity Press.

Antal, C. (2008). Reflections on religious nationalism, conflict and schooling in developing democracies: India and Israel in comparative perspective. *Compare: A Journal of Comparative and International Education, 38*(1), 87–102.

Arendt, H. (1958). *The human condition.* London: The University of Chicago Press.

Arendt, H. (1978). *The life of mind.* New York: Harcourt Brace Jovanovich.

Avila-Saavedra, G. (2013). Neither here nor there: Consumption of US media among pre-adolescent girls in Ecuador. *Interactions: Studies in Communication & Culture, 4*(3), 136–152.

Bakardjieva, M. (2010). The internet and subactivism: Cultivating young citizenship in everyday life. In T. Olsson & P. Dahlgren (Eds.), *Young people, ICTs, and democracy: Theories, policies, identities and websites* (pp. 129–146). Goteborg, Sweden: Nordicom, University of Gothenburg.

Banaji, S. (2015). Behind the high-tech fetish: Children, work and media use across classes in India. *The International Communication Gazette, 77*(6), 577–599.

Banaji, S. (2018). Vigilante publics: Orientalism, modernity and Hindutva fascism in India. *Javnost-The Public, 25*(4), 333–350.

© The Editor(s) (if applicable) and The Author(s), under exclusive license   145
to Springer Nature Switzerland AG 2019
K. V. Bhatia and M. Pathak-Shelat, *Challenging Discriminatory Practices of Religious Socialization among Adolescents,*
https://doi.org/10.1007/978-3-030-29574-5

Barnes, D., & Todd, F. (1978). *Communication and learning in small groups.* London: Routledge.

Bazalgette, C. (1989). *Primary media education: A curriculum statement.* London: British Film Institute.

Bennett, W. L. (2008). Changing citizenship in the digital age. In W. L. Bennett (Ed.), *Civic life online: Learning how digital media can engage youth* (pp. 1–24). Cambridge: MIT Press.

Bhaktin, M. (1981). Discourse in the novel. In M. Holquist (Ed.), *The dialogic imagination: Four essays by M. M. Bakhtin* (pp. 259–422). Austin: University of Texas Press.

Bhaktin, M. (1986). *Speech genres and other late essays.* Austin: University of Texas.

Bhatia, K. (2016). Understanding the role of media education in promoting religious literacy: A critical pedagogy for primary school students in rural India. *Media Education Research Journal, 7*(2), 11–28.

Bhatia, K. (2018). Mediating religious literacy among primary school children in Gujarat: Classrooms as a liminal space. *Journal of Media Literacy Education, 10*(3), 152–170.

Bhatia, K., & Pathak-Shelat, M. (2017). Media literacy as a pathway to religious literacy in pluralistic democracies: Designing a critical media education pedagogy for primary school children in India. *Interactions: Studies in Communication & Culture, 8*(2), 189–209.

Bhatia, K., & Pathak-Shelat, M. (2019). Media experiences in community-driven rural areas: Exploring children's media cultures in rural Gujarat, India. *Journal of Children and Media.* https://doi.org/10.1080/17482798.2019.1616575.

Blühdorn, I. (2006). Self-experience in the theme park of radical action? Social movements and political articulation in the late-modern condition. *European Journal of Social Theory, 9*(1), 23–42.

Blythe, T. (2002). Working hard for the money: A faith-based media literacy analysis of the top television dramas of 2000–2001. *Journal of Media & Religion, 1*(3), 139–151.

Boal, A. (1985). *Theatre of the oppressed.* New York: Theatre Communications Group.

Bourne, J. (2003). Vertical discourse: The role of the teacher in the transmission and acquisition of decontextualized language. *European Education Research Journal, 2*(4), 496–521.

Boyd, D. (2007). Why youth (heart) social network sites: The role of networked publics in teenage social life. In D. Buckingham (Ed.), *MacArthur foundation series on digital learning—Youth, identity and digital media volume* (pp. 119–142). Cambridge: MIT Press.

Braggs, S. (2007). 'Student voice' and governmentality: The production of enterprising subjects? *Discourse: Studies in the Cultural Politics of Education, 28*(3), 343–358.

Braun, V., & Clarke, V. (2006). Using thematic analysis in psychology. *Qualitative Research in Psychology, 3*(2), 77–101.

Brookfield, S. (1994). Tales from the dark side: A phenomenography of adult critical reflection. *International Journal of Lifelong Education, 13*(3), 203–218.

Brown, R., & Renshaw, P. (2006). Positioning students as actors and authors: A chronotopic analysis of collaborative learning activities. *Mind, Culture, and Activity, 13*(3), 247–259.

Buckingham, D. (2003). *Media education: Literacy, learning and contemporary culture.* Cambridge: Polity Press.

Buckingham, D. (2005). *The media literacy of children and young people: A review of literature on behalf of OFCOM* (Project Report). London, UK: OFCOM.

Buckingham, D., Niesyto, H., & Fisherkeller, J. (2003). Videoculture: Crossing borders with young people's video productions. *Television and New Media, 4*(4), 461–482.

Buckingham, D., & Sefton-Green, J. (2003). Gotta catch 'em all: Structure, agency and pedagogy in children's media culture. *Media, Culture & Society, 25*(3), 379–399.

Casquete, J. (2006). The power of demonstration. *Social Movement Studies, 5*(1), 45–60.

Cheng, K. (2009). The times they are a changing: Media education. In C. Cheung (Ed.), *Media education in Asia* (pp. 13–18). Dordrecht: Springer. https://doi.org/10.1007/978-1-4020-9529-0_5.

Collier, S. (2009). Typologies of power: Foucault's analysis of political government beyond 'governmentality'. *Theory, Culture and Society, 26*(6), 78–108.

Conroy, J. (2004). *Betwixt and between: The liminal imagination, education and democracy.* New York: Peter Lang.

Davidson, A. (2011). In praise of counter-conduct. *History of Human Sciences, 24*(4), 25–41.

Davison, R. M., Ou, C., Martinsons, M., Zhao, A., & Du, R. (2014). The communicative ecology of Web 2.0 at work: Social networking in the workspace. *Journal of the Association for Information Science and Technology, 65*(10), 2035–2047.

Davy, C., Magalhaes, L., Mandich, A., & Galheigo, S. (2014). Aspects of the resilience and settlement of refugee youth: A narrative study using body maps. *UFSCar, 22*(2), 231–241.

Dean, M. (1992). A genealogy of the government of poverty. *Economy and Society, 21*(3), 215–251.

Dean, M. (1999). *Governmentality: Power and rule in modern society.* London: Sage.

Death, C. (2010). Counter-conducts: A foucauldian analytics of protest. *Social Movement Studies, 9*(3), 235–251.

de Certeau, M. (1984). *The practices of everyday life.* Los Angeles: University of California Press.

Dery, M. (1993). *Culture jamming: Hacking, slashing and sniping in the empire of signs* (Vol. 25). Westfield: Open Magazine Pamphlet Series.

Devine, C. (2008). The moon, the stars, and a scar: Body mapping stories of women living with HIV/AIDS. *Border Crossings, 27*(2), 58–65.

Dewey, J. (1954). *The public and its problems.* Athens, OH: Swallow Press.

Donnan, H., & Wilson, T. (1999). *Borders: Frontiers of identity, nation and state.* London: Bloomsbury.

Dorrestijn, S. (2012). Technical mediation and subjectivation: Tracing and extending Foucault's philosophy of teaching. *Philosophy & Technology, 25*(2), 221–241.

Drotner, K. (2008). Leisure is hard work: Digital practices and future competencies. In D. Buckingham (Ed.), *Youth, identity and digital media* (pp. 167–184). Cambridge: MIT Press.

Erstad, O., & Gilje, Ø. (2008). Regaining impact: Media education and media literacy in a Norwegian context. *Nordicom Review, 29*(2), 219–230.

Falzon, C. (2013). Foucault, subjectivity, and technologies of the self. In Z. Falzon, T. O'leary, & J. Sawicki (Eds.), *A companion to Foucault* (pp. 510–525). New York: Wiley Blackwell.

Ferreday, D., Hodgson, V., & Jones, C. (2006). Dialogue, language and identity: Critical issues for networked management learning. *Studies in Continuing Education, 28*(3), 223–239.

Fish, S. (1980). *Is there a text in this class.* Cambridge, UK: Harvard University Press.

Fisherkeller, J. E. (1999). Learning about power and success: Young urban adolescents interpret TV culture. *Communication Review, 3*(3), 187–199.

Fleetwood, N. (2005). Authenticating practices: Producing realness, performing youth. In S. Maira & E. Seop (Eds.), *Youthscapes: The popular, the national, the global* (pp. 155–172). Philadelphia: University of Pennsylvania Press.

Foth, M., & Hearn, G. (2007). Networked individualism of urban residents: Discovering the communicative ecology in inner-city apartment buildings. *Information, Communication & Society, 10*(5), 749–772.

Foucault, M. (1970). *The order of things: An archaeology of the human sciences.* New York: Pantheon Books.

Foucault, M. (1972). *The archaeology of knowledge* (Alan M. Sheridan Smith, Trans.). New York: Pantheon Books.

Foucault, M. (1973). *The birth of the clinic: An archaeology of medical perception.* London: Routledge.

Foucault, M. (1978). *The history of sexuality, volume 1: An introduction* (R. Hurley, Trans.). New York: Pantheon Books.

Foucault, M. (1980). Power/knowledge. In *Selected interviews and other writings 1972–1977.* Brighton: The Harvester Press.

Foucault, M. (1982). The subject and power. *Critical Inquiry, 8*(4), 777–795.

Foucault, M. (1988). Technologies of the self. In L. H. Martin, H. Gutman, & P. H. Hutton (Eds.), *Technologies of the self: A seminar with Michel Foucault* (pp. 16–49). London: Tavistock.

Foucault, M. (1997). *Discipline and punish: The birth of the prison* (A. Sheridan, Trans.). New York: Random House.

Foucault, M. (2003). *Society must be defended': Lectures at the Collège de France 1975–1976*. New York: Picador.

Foucault, M. (2007). *Security, territory, population: Lectures at the Colle'ge de France 1977–1978*. Basingstoke: Palgrave Macmillan.

Frau-Meigs, D., & Torrent, J. (2009). Media education policy: Toward a global rationale. In D. Frau-Meigs & J. Torrent (Eds.), *Mapping media education policies in the world* (pp. 15-21). New York: UN Alliance of Civilizations.

Freire, P. (1970). *Pedagogy of the oppressed*. New Delhi: Penguin Books.

Freire, P. (1973). *Education for critical consciousness*. New York, NY: Seabury Press.

Freire, P. (1976). *Education, the practice of freedom*. New York: Writers and Readers Publishing Cooperative.

Garlough, C. (2008). On the political uses of folklore: Performance and grassroots feminist activism in India. *The Journal of American Folklore, 121*(480), 167–191.

Gee, J. (2003). *What video game have to teach us about learning and literacy*. New York: Palgrave Macmillan.

Geiger, W. (2001). Talk about TV: Television viewers' interpersonal communication about programming. *Communication Reports, 14*(1), 49–59.

Ghatak, S., & Abel, A. (2013). Power/faith: Governmentality, religion, and post-secular societies. *International Journal of Politics, Culture, and Society, 26*(3), 217–235.

Giddens, A. (1984). *The constitution of society*. Cambridge, UK: Polity Press.

Giroux, H. (1987). Critical literacy and student experience: Donald Graves' approach to literacy. *Language Arts, 64*(2), 175–181.

Giroux, H. (1988). *Teachers as intellectuals: Toward a critical pedagogy of learning*. New York: Bergin and Garvey.

Giroux, H. (2001). *Public spaces, private lives: Beyond the culture of cynicism*. Lanham, MD: Rowman & Littlefield.

Giroux, H. A. (1992). *Border crossings: Cultural workers and the politics of education*. New York: Routledge.

Giroux, H. A. (1994). *Disturbing pleasures: Learning popular culture*. New York: Routledge.

Goldfarb, B. (2002). *Visual pedagogy: Media cultures in and beyond the classroom*. Durham: Duke University Press.

Goldstein, R. (2007). The perilous pitfalls of praxis: Critical pedagogy as "regime of truth". In R. Goldstein (Ed.), *Useful theory: Making critical education practical* (pp. 15–29). New York: Peter Lang.

Hall, S. (1994). Culture identity and diaspora. In P. William & L. Chrisman (Eds.), *Colonial discourse and post-colonial theory: A reader* (pp. 392–403). New York: Columbia University Press.

Hart, A. (2001). Awkward practice: Teaching media in English. *Changing English, 8*(1), 65–81.

Hearn, N., & Foth, M. (2007). Communicative ecologies: Editorial preface. *Electronic Journal of Communication, 17,* 1–2.

Held, D. (2002). The transformation of political community: Rethinking democracy in the context of globalization. In N. Dower & J. Williams (Eds.), *Global citizenship: A critical introduction* (pp. 92–100). New York: Routledge.

Heller, K. (1996). Power, subjectification and resistance in Foucault. *SubStance, 25*(1), 78–110.

Henderson, L. (2009, March). Let's all be neighbours on Will Wright Street. *Walrus Magazine,* pp. 56–58.

Hill, J. (2011). Endangered childhoods: How consumerism is impacting child and youth identity. *Media, Culture & Society, 33*(3), 347–362.

Hobbs, R. (1998). The seven great debates in the media literacy movement. *Journal of Communication, 48*(1), 16–32.

Hobbs, R. (2004). A review of school-based initiatives in media literacy education. *American Behavioral Scientist, 48*(1), 42–59.

Hobbs, R. (2008). Debates and challenges facing new literacies in the 21st century. In K. Drotner & S. Livingstone (Eds.), *The international handbook of children, media and culture* (pp. 431–447). London: Sage.

Hobbs, R., & Jensen, A. (2009). The past, present and future of media literacy education. *The Journal of Media Literacy Education, 1*(1), 1–11.

Hoechsmann, M., & Poyntz, S. (2012). *Media literacies: A critical introduction.* Chichester: Wiley-Blackwell.

Hoggart, R. (1957). *The uses of literacy.* Fairlawn: Essential Books.

Howard, R. (2005). A theory of vernacular rhetoric: The case of the "Sinner's Prayer" online. *Folklore, 116*(2), 172–188.

Hutchings, K. (2002). Feminism and global citizenship. In N. Dower & J. Williams (Eds.), *Global citizenship: A critical introduction* (pp. 30–40). New York: Routledge.

Jain, A. (2010). Beaming it live: 24-hour television news, the spectator and the spectacle of the 2002 Gujarat carnage. *South Asian Popular Culture, 8*(2), 163–179.

Jankowski, N. (2002). Creating community with media: History, theories and scientific investigations. In L. S. Lievrouw & S. M. Livingstone (Eds.), *Handbook of new media: Social shaping and consequences of ICTs* (pp. 34–49). Thousand Oaks: Sage.

Jayal, N. G. (2001). *Democracy and the state: Welfare, secularism and development in contemporary India.* New Delhi: Oxford University Press.

Jenkins, H., Clinton, K., Purushotma, R., Robinson, A., & Weigel, M. (2006). *Confronting the challenges of participatory culture.* New York: New York University Press.

Jenkins, H., Ford, S., & Green, J. (2013). *Spreadable media: Creating value and meaning in a network culture.* New York: New York University Press.

Jenkins, H., Shresthova, S., Gamber-Thompson, L., Kligler-Vilenchik, N., & Zimmerman, A. (2016). *By any media necessary: The new youth activism.* New York, NY: New York University Press.

Johnson, R. (1986–1987). What is cultural studies anyway? *Social Text, 16,* 38–80.

Jolls, T., & Wilson, C. (2014). The core concepts; Fundamental to media literacy yesterday, today and tomorrow. *Journal of Media Literacy Education, 6*(2), 68–78.

Jonassen, D., Carr, C., & Yueh, H. (1998). Computers as mindtools for engaging learners in critical thinking. *TechTrends, 43*(2), 24–32.

Jordan, M. (2015). *Convulsing bodies: Religion and resistance in Foucault.* Stanford, CA: Stanford University Press.

Kanpol, B. (1992). Postmodernism in education revisited: Similarities within differences and the democratic imaginary. *Educational Theory, 42*(2), 217–230.

Kellner, D. (1998). Multiple literacies and critical pedagogy in a multicultural society. *Educational Theory, 48*(1), 103–123.

Kellner, D. (2002). Critical perspectives on visual literacy in media and cyberculture. *Journal of Visual Literacy, 22*(1), 81–90.

Kenway, J., & Bullen, E. (2008). The global corporate curriculum and the young cyberflaneur as global citizen. In N. Dolby & F. Rizvi (Eds.), *Youth moves: Identities and education in global perspective* (pp. 17–32). New York: Routledge.

Kirmani, N. (2008). Competing constructions of "Muslim-ness" in the South Delhi neighborhood of Zakir Nagar. *Journal of Muslim Minority Affairs, 28*(3), 355–370.

Kubey, R. (2003). Why U.S. media education lags behind the rest of the English speaking world. *Television New Media, 4*(4), 351–370.

Lallement, M. (2014). Foucault's biopolitics: A critique of ontology. *Journal of the British Society for Phenomenology, 43*(1), 76–91.

Land, R., Rattray, J., & Vivian, P. (2014). Learning in the liminal space: A semiotic approach to threshold concepts. *Higher Education, 67*(2), 199–217.

Lankshear, C. (1997). *Changing literacies, changing education.* New York: Open University Press.

Lave, J., & Wenger, E. (1991). *Situated learning: Legitimate peripheral participation.* Cambridge: Cambridge University Press.

Lemish, D. (2015). *Children and media: A global perspective.* Oxford: Wiley Blackwell.

Lemke, T. (2001). The birth of biopolitics: Michel Foucault's lecture at the Collège de France on neo-liberal government. *Economy and Society, 30,* 190–207.

Lennie, J., & Tacchi, J. (2013). *Evaluating communication for development: A framework for social change.* Abingdon: Routledge.

Leone, M. (2004). *Religious conversion and identity: Semiotic analysis of texts.* New York: Routledge.

Lewis, J., & Jhally, S. (1998). The struggle over media literacy. *Journal of Communication, 48*(1), 1–8.

Linell, P. (1998). *Approaching dialogue: Talk, interaction and contexts in dialogic perspective.* Amsterdam: Benjamins.

Linell, P. (2003). *What is dialogism? Aspects and elements of a dialogical approach to language, communication and cognition.* Retrieved December 31, 2017 from http://www.tema.liu.se/tema-k/personal/perli/What-is-dialogism.pdf.

Littleton, K., Mercer, N., Dawes, L., Wegerif, R., Rowe, D., & Sams, C. (2005). Talking and thinking together at key stage 1. *Early Years: An International Journal of Research and Development, 25*(2), 67–182.

Livingstone, S. (2009). *Children and the internet: Great expectations, challenging realities.* Cambridge: Polity Press.

Livingstone, S., & Haddon, L. (2009). *Young people in the European digital media landscape: A statistical overview.* Goteborg, Sweden: International Clearinghouse on Children, Youth and Media.

Lorenzini, D. (2016). From counter-conduct to critical attitude: Michel Foucault and the art of not being governed quite so much. *Foucault Studies, 21,* 7–21.

Luke, C. (2002). Cyber-schooling and technological change: Multiple literacies for new times. In B. Cope & M. Kalantzis (Eds.), *Multiliteracies: Literacy learning and the design of social futures* (pp. 69–91). London: Routledge.

Macgregor, N. H. (2009). Mapping the body: Tracing the personal and the political dimensions of HIV/AIDs in Khayelitsha, South Africa. *Anthropology & Medicine, 16*(1), 85–95.

Malmvig, H. (2016). Eyes wide shut: Power and creative counter-conducts in the battle for Syria, 2011–2014. *Global society.* https://doi.org/10.1080/13600826.2016.1150810.

Martens, H. (2010). Evaluating media literacy education: Concepts, theories, and future directions. *Journal of Media Literacy Education, 2,* 1–22.

Mason, B. (1992). *Street theatre and other outdoor performance.* London, UK: Routledge.

Masterman, L. (1985). *Teaching the media.* London: Comedia Publishing Group.

McDougall, J. (2014). Media literacy: An incomplete project. In B. De Abreu & P. Mihailidis (Eds.), *Media literacy education in action: Theoretical and pedagogical perspectives* (pp. 3–10). New York: Routledge.

McLaren, P. (1995). *Critical pedagogy and predatory culture: Oppositional politics in a postmodern era.* New York, NY: Routledge.

Meikle, G. (2007). Stop signs: An introduction to culture jamming. In K. Coyer, T. Dowmunt, & A. Fountain (Eds.), *The alternative media handbook* (pp. 166–179). London: Routledge.

Mercer, N. (2000). *Words and minds: How we use language to think together.* London: Routledge.

Merleau-Ponty, M. (1964). *The visible and the invisible* (C. Lefort, Ed. and A. Lingis, Trans.). Evanston: Northwestern University Press.

Meyer, J., & Land, R. (2005). *Overcoming barriers to student understanding: Threshold concepts and troublesome knowledge.* London and New York: Routledge.

Meyrowitz, J. (1984). The adultlike child and the childlike adult: Socialization in an electronic world. *Daedalus, 113*(3), 19–48.

Mill, J. S. M. (1977). On liberty. In J. M. Robson (Ed.), *The collected works of John Stuart Mill* (Vol. XVIII). Toronto and London: University of Toronto Press.

Nussbaum, M. (2007). *The clash within: Democracy, religious violence, and India's future.* Cambridge: Harvard University Press.

O'Brien, S., & Szeman, I. (2004). *Popular culture: A user's guide.* Scarborough: Nelson.

O'Neill, K. (2004). Transnational protest: States, circuses, and conflicts at the frontline of global politics. *International Studies Review, 6*(2), 233–251.

Oring, E. (2008). Legendary and the rhetoric of truth. *Journal of American Folklore, 121*(480), 127–166.

Orner, M. (1992). Interrupting the calls for student voice in libratory education: A feminist poststructuralist perspective. In C. Luke & J. Gore (Eds.), *Feminisms and critical pedagogy* (pp. 15–25). New York: Routledge.

Pathak-Shelat, M. (2014). *Global civic engagement on online platforms: Women as transcultural citizens* (Unpublished dissertation). University of Wisconsin-Madison, Madison.

Pathak-Shelat, M., & DeShano, C. (2013). Digital youth cultures in small town and rural Gujarat, India. *New Media and Society, 16*(6), 983–1001.

Patton, P. (1989). Taylor and Foucault on power and freedom. *Political Studies, 37*(2), 260–276.

Potter, W. J. (2004). Argument for the need for a cognitive theory of media literacy. *American Behavioral Scientist, 48*(2), 266–272.

Poyntz, S. (2006). Independent media, youth agency, and the promise of media education. *Canadian Journal of Education, 29*(1), 154–175.

Poyntz, S. (2015). Conceptual futures: Thinking and the role of key concept models in media literacy education. *Media Education Research Journal, 6*(1), 63–79.

Pratt, M. (1992). Arts of the contact zone. *Modern Language Association, 5*(8), 33–40.

Prentki, T., & Selman, J. (2000). *Popular theatre in political culture: Britain and Canada in focus.* Bristol: Intellect Books.

Rangaswamy, N., Nair, S., & Toyama, K. (2008). "My TV is the family oven/toaster/grill": Personalizing TV for the Indian audience. In Proceeding of the 1st International Conference on Designing Interactive User Experiences for TV and Video—uxtv '08. Silicon Valley, CA, USA.

Rajagopal, A. (2001). *Politics after television: Hindu nationalism and the reshaping of the public in India.* Cambridge: Cambridge University Press.

Reynolds, M. (1999). Grasping the nettle: Possibilities and pitfalls of a critical management pedagogy. *British Journal of Management, 10*(2), 171–184.

Ricouer, P. (1981). *Hermeneutics and the human sciences.* Cambridge: Cambridge University Press.

Rojas Drummond, S., Fernandez, M., Mazon, N., & Wegerif, R. (2006). Collaborative talk and creativity. *Teaching Thinking and Creativity, 1*(2), 84–94.

Rommetveit, R. (1992). Outlines of a dialogically based social-cognitive approach to human cognition and communication. In A. Wold (Ed.), *The dialogic alternative: Towards a theory of language and mind* (pp. 19–45). Oslo: Scandinavian Press.

Rose, N. (1996). Governing advanced liberal democracies. In A. Barry, T. Osborne, & N. Rose (Eds.), *Foucault and political reason: Liberalism, neo-liberalism and rationalities of government* (pp. 37–64). London: UCL Press.

Rose, N. (1999). *Powers of freedom: Reframing political thought.* Cambridge: Cambridge University Press.

Sams, C., Wegerif, R., Dawes, L., & Mercer, N. (2005). *Thinking together with ICT and primary mathematics: A continuing professional development pack.* London: SMILE Mathematics.

Sawin, P. (2002). Performance at the nexus of gender, power, and desire: Reconsidering Bauman's verbal art from the perspective of gendered subjectivity as performance. *Journal of American Folklore, 115*(455), 28–61.

Scharrer, E. (2002). Making a case for media literacy in the curriculum: Outcomes and assessment. *Journal of Adolescent & Adult Literacy, 46*(4), 354–358.

Scharrer, E. (2006). Sixth graders take on television: Media literacy and critical attitudes of television violence. *Communication Research Reports, 22*(1), 325–333.

Scheibe, C. L. (2004). A deeper sense of literacy: Curriculum-driven approaches to media literacy in the K-12 classroom. *American Behavioral Scientist, 48*(1), 60–68.

Schwartzman, L. (2010). Transcending disciplinary boundaries: A proposed theoretical foundation for threshold concepts. In J. H. F. Meyer, R. Land, & C. Baillie (Eds.), *Threshold concepts and transformational learning* (pp. 21–44). Rotterdam: Sense Publishing.

Sefton-Green, J. (2006). Youth, technology and media cultures. *Review of Research in Education, 30*, 279–306.

Sikand, Y. (2008). *Issues in madrasa education in India.* New Delhi: Hope India Publications.

Silverstone, R. (2007). *Media and morality: On the rise of the Mediapolis.* Cambridge: Polity Press.

Simons, M., & Masschelein, J. (2011). Governmental, political and pedagogic subjectivation: Foucault with Ranciere. In M. Simon & J. Masschelein (Eds.), *Ranciere, public education and the taming of democracy* (pp. 76–92). Sydney: Philosophy of Education Society of Australia.

Slater, D. (2013). *New media, development and gobalization: Making connections in the global south.* Cambridge: Polity Press.

Smyth, J. W. (1987). *A rationale for teachers' critical pedagogy: A handbook.* Geelong, VIC: Deakin University.

Soep, E. (2006). Beyond literacy and voice in youth media education. *McGill Journal of Education, 41*(3), 197–213.

Sokhi-Bulley, B. (2016). Re-reading the riots: Counter-conduct in London 2011. *Global Society.* https://doi.org/10.1080/13600826.2016.1143348.

Srampickal, J. (1990). *Voice to the voiceless.* New York: St. Martin.

St John, G. (2008). Protestival: Global days of action and carnalivalized politics in the present. *Social Movement Studies, 7*(2), 167–190.

Stingl, A. (2011). Truth, knowledge, narratives of selves: An account of the volatility of truth, the power of semantic agency, and time in narratives of the self. *The American Sociologist, 42*(2/3), 207–219.

Stout, D. A. (2002). Religious media literacy: Toward a research agenda. *Journal of Media & Religion, 1*(1), 49.

Sud, N. (2009). Secularism and the Gujarat state: 1960–2005. *Modern Asian Studies, 42*(6), 1251–1281.

Sud, N. (2012). *Liberalization, Hindu nationalism and the state: A biography of Gujarat.* New Delhi: Oxford University Press.

Sun, F., & Scharrer, E. (2004). Staying true to Disney: College students' resistance to criticism of The Little Mermaid. *Communication Review, 7*(1), 35–55.

Valsamidis, P. (2016). Representing "Us"—Representing "Them": Visualizing racism in Greek primary school films. In J. Singh, P. Kerr, & E. Hamburger (Eds.), *Media and information literacy: Reinforcing human rights, countering radicalization and extremism* (pp. 213–222). Paris: UNESCO.

Velde, J. (2012). *From liminal to liminoid: Eminem's trickstering.* Bergen: University of Bergen.

Wegerif, R. (2007). *Dialogic education and teaching: Expanding the space of learning.* New York: Springer.

Wegerif, R., & Mercer, N. (2000). Language for thinking. In M. Cowie, D. Aalsvoort, & N. Mercer (Eds.), *New perspectives in collaborative learning.* Oxford: Elsevier.

Wegerif, R., Perez Linares, J., Rojas Drummond, S., Mercer, N., & Velez, M. (2005). Thinking together in the UK and Mexico: Transfer of an educational innovation. *Journal of Classroom Interaction, 40*(1), 199–211.

Weir, L. (2008). The concept of truth. *The Canadian Journal of Sociology, 33*(2), 367–389.

Wenger, E. (1999). *Communities of practice: Learning, meaning and identity.* Cambridge, UK: Cambridge University Press.

Westheimer, J., & Kahne, J. (2004). What kind of citizens? The politics of educating for democracy. *American Educational Research Journal, 41*(2), 237–269.

Willet, R. (2008). Consumer citizens online: Structure, agency, and gender in online participation. In D. Buckingham (Ed.), *Youth, identity and digital media* (pp. 49–69). Cambridge: MIT Press.

Williams, R. (1958). *Culture and society, 1780–1950.* New York: Columbia.

Williamson, K. M., & Brown, K. (2014). Collective voices: Engagement of Hartford community residents through participatory action research. *The Qualitative Report, 19*(36), 1–14.

Youdell, D. (2006). Subjectivation and performative politics: Butler thinking Althusser and Foucault: Intelligibility, agency and the raced-nationed-religioned subjects of education. *British Journal of Sociology of Religion, 27*(4), 511–528.

INDEX